CONCILIUM

Religion in the Seventies

CONCILIUM
Religion in the Seventies

EDITORIAL DIRECTORS: Edward Schillebeeckx (Dogma) • Herman Schmidt (Liturgy) • Alois Müller (Pastoral) • Hans Küng (Ecumenisn) • Franz Böckle (Moral Theology) • Johannes B. Metz (Church and World) • Roger Aubert (Church History) • Teodoro Jiménez Urresti (Canon Law) • Christian Duquoc (Spirituality) • Pierre Benoît and Roland Murphy (Scripture)

CONSULTING EDITORS: Marie-Dominique Chenu • ✠Carlo Colombo • Yves Congar • Andrew Greely • Jorge Mejía • Karl Rahner • Roberto Tucci

EXECUTIVE SECRETARY: (Awaiting new appointment), Arksteestraat 3–5, Nijmegen, The Netherlands

Volume 78: Canon Law

EDITORIAL BOARD: William Bassett • Peter Huizing • Manuel Bonet Muixi • Michael Breydy • Albertus Eysink • Tomás García Barberena • Antonio García y García • Jean Gaudemet • Johannes Gerhartz • Teodoro Jiménez Urresti • Cornelis de Jong • Gonzalez Martinez Diez • Paul Mikat • Charles Munier • Johannes Neumann • Ladislas Orsy • Juan Radrizzani • Giovanni Řezáč • Robert Soullard • Luis Vela Sanchez

CELIBACY IN THE CHURCH

Edited by
William Bassett
and Peter Huizing

Herder and Herder

1972
HERDER AND HERDER NEW YORK
1221 Avenue of the Americas,
New York 10020

ISBN: 07–073608–1

Cum approbatione Ecclesiastica

Library of Congress Catalog Card Number: 72–3943

Printed in the United States

CONTENTS

PART II

DOCUMENTATION

Editorial

THE present number of *Concilium* fulfils a promise made by the editors three years ago to devote an entire issue to a study of ministry and celibacy in the Church. Much has happened in this time to sharpen the focus of a debate that has continued universally over a decade and shows no signs of abating. In the time of preparation for the Synod of Bishops in 1971 many episcopal conferences commissioned research and engaged in extensive consultation regarding the present mandatory relationship between ministry and celibacy in the Roman Catholic Church. The sessions in Rome revealed a great sensitivity to this profound human problem in the Church. The deliberations thus involved far more than merely the communication of proposals by representatives of the conferences to the Pope. The record of the Synod indicates that the episcopal college itself accepted the responsibility for decisions to meet the needs of the faithful in the present extreme crisis of the priesthood. The synodal document on the ministerial priesthood was published together with that on justice in the world on 30 November 1971. A papal rescript of that date conveys Pope Paul's acceptance and confirmation of the conclusions of these documents.

The Pope and synodal fathers reaffirmed the law of priestly celibacy existing in the Latin Church. In so doing, however, they suggested the possibility of ordaining married men when, in the judgment of a pope, pastoral needs and the good of the universal Church require it. The documents state a principle which links the pastoral ministry with a life of service. This service in turn should be characterized by total availability to the faithful and Christ-like self-sacrifice. These two conclusions and the sustaining principle of service should be seen in the context of the Church's contemporary experience and the imperative of its mission.

Experience and necessity suggest two factors that bear directly upon the well-being of the universal Church. The first is the fact that hundreds of married men have now received holy orders to exercise a diaconal ministry in the Latin Church. This ministry demands ideally the same availability, selfless devotion and witness that may be expected of priests. Holy orders and a celibate life are no longer necessarily connected in fact in the Latin rite for the first time in centuries. The exercise of holy orders by these married men should be welcomed without reservation. Secondly, as ecumenical dialogue progresses towards broader doctrinal consensus, multiple ministries exercised in the Church by married persons, including the ministries of priest and bishop, must be expected. Plans must be made to provide that Catholics accept and appreciate the ministries of ordained married people. Concern for the ideal of celibacy in our tradition cannot obscure the need to prepare now for flexibility in the life styles not only of deacons, but of priests and bishops in the re-united Christianity towards which we strive. The married bishops and priests of the Churches of the East and West form a major segment of the total Christian ministry. The closer Catholics draw to these Churches the more necessary it is to accept this fact and see its eventual influence on the shape of the Church. While it is true that celibacy will remain a respected Christian ideal for many, it is no longer in fact or in expectation the absolute rule of the ordained ministry.

A radical and sudden change in an institution with a centuries-long history should not be expected. Indeed, pastoral prudence dictates caution and a great sensitivity to the feelings of the Catholic faithful. Yet the tradition of the past cannot blind us to the urgency of the present and the need to prepare the modifications in the regulations prohibiting the marriage of priests and bishops we must expect in the future.

The studies presented here are not just another in an already crowded list of publications on celibacy and ministry. They were carefully prepared and discussed over two years to provide a plan, to illustrate difficulties and make practical suggestions for a responsible preparation for change for the good of the Church. Planning and counselling to meet foreseeable eventualities form part of the lawyer's art. Combining the results of scholarly inter-disciplinary and ecumenical reflection to draw practical con-clusions for the life of Christians is the duty of the canonist. Reading the signs of the times with careful discernment to pre-pare for development in the future is precisely the tradition be-hind the creative methodology of the science of canon law.

Movements of general reform in the Church since the thir-teenth century have involved a persistent plea for renewal of the liturgy and of the ministry. Once the polemic bitterness of the Reformation had been transcended and substantial theological and pastoral development had illumined the way to enhance essential Christian values for our day, proposals for renewal were accepted and are now being implemented. A vernacular liturgy and the restoration of the reception of the Holy Eucharist under both species today highlight an immensely beneficial revitaliza-tion of the Church's sacramental life. In like manner, we may confidently expect a renewal of ministry in a new freedom and variety of life styles and flexibility of service. The gift of celibacy accepted for the sake of the kingdom of God among men is re-spected now and admired. Christians can see and be grateful for this extraordinary grace in the Church. No doubt it will perdure; indeed, according to the needs of the times the celibate witness will spread and become increasingly effective. But by the same token we also see now much more benefit than we were aware of in the past from a priesthood exercised by those free to be mar-ried or celibate.

The first section of essays illustrates historical changes in the Christian significance of celibacy for ministry and the good reasons why many Christians feel a law of mandatory celibacy is inappropriate. The second group of essays points to the difficult problems involved in any period of transition. These lead to a final plan for a process of canonical development to effect a sure and salutary reform of ministry and celibacy for pastoral needs and the good of the universal Church. Three bulletins detail the sentiments and expectations of Catholics around the world.

A plan for the renewal of ministry in the Catholic Church has but a single purpose: to provide the faithful with mature, dedicated and truly God-centred men in the orders of deacon, priest and bishop. We hope these labours will be of benefit to our readers, especially those who bear the heavy responsibility of decision among the people of God.

WILLIAM BASSETT
PETER HUIZING

PART I
ARTICLES

Gerard Sloyan

Biblical and Patristic Motives for Celibacy of Church Ministers

BASIC to the development of celibacy for Christian ministers was the biblical prescription of abstention from sexual activity by Jewish priests for a period before their service, and a similar taboo for participants in a holy war. Peter the Lombard relies on the assumption that there exists an unbroken link between the Aaronic priesthood of the Hebrew Scriptures and the Christian priesthood.[1] The continuator of Aquinas does the same.[2] This tradition, which is not primitive, goes back to a time no earlier than the third century.

The New Testament presents the institution of priesthood as radicalized in Christ. The solidarity of the priesthood in Israel became the solidarity of the Spirit in the life of the Church. "One of the truly revolutionary claims and characteristics of the early Church," writes Bishop Robinson, "was what it called the 'common ownership', the *koinonia*, of Holy Spirit. Hitherto the 'holy' had been defined as that which was not 'common'—and 'the holy' was the sphere of the priest. With the communalization of the holy went the communalization of the priesthood."[3]

[1] *Sent. IV*, d. 24, 9.
[2] "That is designated a holy order which is centred upon something consecrated. Thus there are only three holy orders, namely priesthood and diaconate both of which are concerned with the body of Christ and his consecrated blood, and subdiaconate which is concerned with consecrated vessels. Continence is indicated in each of these cases, so that those who deal with holy things may be holy and pure." *S. Th., Supplementum*, 37, 2 *in corp.*
[3] John A. T. Robinson, "The Priesthood of the Church", in *On Being the Church in the World* (Philadelphia, 1960), p. 76.

The chief characteristic of the leadership class in Israel was the possession of "spirit", as in the case of the seventy prophesying elders (Num. 11. 25). Moses had to name God-fearing and trustworthy men to help him in executing justice (cf. Ex. 18. 21 f.; Deut. 34. 9). The Priestly account of this designation is much longer and has Joshua subjected to the priest Eleazar in all that he should do (cf. Num. 27. 15–23).[4]

The distinction between priest and layman in Israel is a feature of the Priestly writings almost exclusively (cf. Ex. 29. 33; 30. 33). The priest inhabits a sacred sphere. No layman may eat of the sacred food that is the priest's by way of offering (cf. Lev. 22. 20–25). To do so is to engage in profanation (verse 6). A "state of uncleanness" disqualifies any son of Aaron from approaching the sacred offerings. Biblical "leprosy", any flow, any contact with a corpse, with contagion or a "swarming creature", and emission of seed constitute a priest ritually unclean until he bathes himself in water and waits until sundown (cf. Lev. 22. 4–7).

A priest was made holy and sacred by virtue of his work. He was "set apart" (cf. Num. 8. 14; Deut. 10. 8; 1 Chr. 23. 13), this being the root meaning of the tri-literal *ḳadash*.[5] He had left the profane world and entered the sacred realm. He had to tread on sacred ground, handle sacred objects and eat gifts offered in sacrifice.[6]

Members of the priestly line in Israel were subject to special restrictions regarding marriage. "A priest shall not marry a woman who has been a prostitute (*zanah*) or has lost her honour, nor a woman who has been divorced by her husband, for the priest is sacred (*ḳadosh*) to his God" (Lev. 21. 7). This prohibition occurs in a chapter that equates sacredness with conformity to taboos concerning proximity to corpses, the trimming of the hair and beard, the baring of the head and the rending of garments. The separate treatment of God's minister in a variety of matters underlies the prescription as to whom the "most exalted of the priests" (*ha ḳohen ha gadol*, verse 10) may marry, namely a

---

[4] Cf. Joseph Blenkinsopp, *Celibacy, Ministry, Church* (New York, 1968), p. 106.

[5] Gesenius-Richardson, *A Hebrew and English Lexicon of the Old Testament* (Oxford, 1952, 1907), s.v., p. 871.

[6] Roland de Vaux, *Ancient Israel* (New York, 1961), p. 348.

virgin (verses 13 f.). Since priestly widows have been "consecrated" by their first marriage, they are fit candidates to marry priests.

Ezekiel 44 is devoted in its entirety to the priest's office (cf. verse 23) of distinguishing between the sacred (*kodesh*) and the profane (*chol*), the unclean (*tameh*) and the clean (*tahor*). Holiness and its opposite, uncleanness, are thought of as physical and communicable, e.g., in the prescription that the priests are to wear linen drawers and nothing that causes sweat (cf. Ez. 44. 18 f).

These notions of holiness and impurity are unrelated to ethical virtue or fault. Under discussion, rather, are " 'states' or 'conditions' from which men must emerge in order to re-enter normal life".[7] The various interdicts and rituals for purification and desecration were derived from archaic customs of uncertain origin. They were incorporated into the Priestly legislation, the latest part of the Pentateuch, and given a new meaning in the interests of separating Israel from the pagan world around it. Washing was the normal way for a priest to rid himself of impurity and safely enter the realm of the sacred (cf. Ex. 29. 4; 30. 17–21; Lev. 8. 6; 16. 4).

In the concept of the holy war, continence was prescribed for the participants (cf. 1 Sam. 21. 6). David was led to the extremity of putting Uriah in the front line of battle because, having slept with Uriah's wife, he could not persuade this pious warrior to break the terms of combat by going home for a night (cf. 2 Sam. 11. 6–15). The requirements of ritual cleanliness in combat were not restricted to intercourse. They extended to nocturnal emission, which had to be corrected by self-removal from the camp and ritual bathing before one could be readmitted (cf. Deut. 23. 11). This behaviour was thought to be required by the fact that Israel's wars were the wars of Yahweh. The camp "had to be kept 'holy' if Yahweh was to encamp with his troops (Deut. 23. 10–15".[8]

The legislation on the holy war is noted here because of the use made by Christians of the passage in Mk. 2. 25 ff. and parallels which cite 1 Sam. 21. 2–8 in support of the notion of sexual abstention as a condition for eating the holy (i.e., eucharistic) bread. In context in 1 Sam., the ritual purity that David claimed

---

[7] de Vaux, *op. cit.*, p. 460.
[8] *Ibid.*, p. 259.

for his men extended to all human activity and was not confined
to satisfying hunger through eating sacred food.

When Israel is being constituted a "kingdom of priests" the
whole people is commanded to wash its garments and remain im-
mobile for a brief period: "Be ready for the third day. Have no
intercourse with any woman" (Ex. 19. 15). The underlying notion
seems to be that semen, like sweat or the menstrual flow (cf.
Lev. 15. 18–19), is the defiling agent. The ritually fit person is
not so much the one who has abstained from engaging in sex as
the one on whose body (or clothing) there remains no trace of
such engagement. That is because the sacred is that realm in
which the conditions of human ordinariness—including sexual
intercourse—are suspended.

Philo, Josephus and Pliny the Elder have recorded the abstention of certain segments of the Essene community from sex and
marriage. Such views have been brought in question by the scrolls
of Qumrân and the evidence of its cemetery, where the remains
of women have been found. Nowhere is any such asceticism
attested to or even implied in the texts so far published. *The
Manual of Discipline* does not mention abstention from marriage.
The Damascus Rule (*Zadokite Fragments*) recovered from three
of the Qumrân caves in two slightly varying manuscripts takes
for granted marrying and begetting children.[9]

The only surprise contained in the scrolls is the deferment of
marriage until the age of twenty in a culture that used puberty
as the norm.[10] *The War Rule* has the expected prohibition of
women from the war camps, of anyone maimed, or a man who
has a bodily discharge.[11]. There is no question of the forswearing
of marriage, leading one to wonder if Philo, Josephus and Pliny
are reporting on this group or on some other infected by neo-
Pythagorean dualism.[12] There is the possibility of foreign influence, whether Greek or Persian, on this sect, just as there was
on other Jewish groups of the time.

Any exceptions to the Jewish practice of universal marriage in

[9] DR A, VII. Vermes, *The Dead Sea Scrolls in English* (Harmonds-
worth, 1968), pp. 103 ff.

[10] MR, I. *Ibid.*, p. 119.

[11] WR, VII. *Ibid.*, p. 133.

[12] Cf. Matthew Black, *The Scrolls and Christian Origins* (New York,
1961), p. 29, n. 1, quoting S. Kraus, *Talmudische Archäologie*, 2, p. 23

fulfilment of the biblical command, "Be fertile and multiply" (Gen. 1. 28), would be noteworthy as background to the New Testament, which in places seems to challenge that universality. It is worth remarking, before proceeding to the New Testament, that the Scrolls establish no extraordinary relation between sexual abstention and priesthood, and the Qumranites were a priestly sect.

It was assumed by the rabbis of Jesus' day and afterwards that the Torah rejected celibacy. Such dualistic asceticism had no currency in rabbinic circles.[13] We do not know why Jesus remained unmarried but can deduce that, on his own principle, it was "for the sake of God's reign" (Mt. 19. 12).[14] Neither do we know what he meant to teach his followers, taken in their entirety, by his abstention. The approbation of the institution of marriage attributed to him in Mark 10. 2–12, however, is unequivocal, when he cites Gen. 1. 27 and couples with it Gen. 2. 24. In his rejection of divorce, Jesus is in a direct line with those biblical teachers who began to make divorce more difficult than in Moses' day (Deut. 24. 1), with its requirement that there be "something indecent" in the woman as a cause for divorce and Malachi's protest in 2. 13–16 against the irresponsible use of divorce in the post-exilic community, probably in the interest of favourable alliances with the semi-pagan people of the land; also the increasing warnings against sexual laxity by the wisdom teachers, e.g., Prov. 2. 16 f.; 6. 24–29; Job 31. 1–9 f.; Wis. 3. 13–16; Sir. 7. 19; 9. 5).

Despite Jesus' teaching on the permanence and indissoluble

[13] Cf. Allan Lazaroff, "Bahyā's Asceticism against its Rabbinic and Islamic Background", *The Journal of Jewish Studies* (1971), p. 33: "For the Rabbis marriage was an unconditional duty. There is only one known instance of a celibate Rabbi. In T. Jeb[amoth] 8, 4 we are told that Ben 'Azzai remained unmarried. He justified his attitude in these words: 'My soul cleaves to the Torah; there is no time for marriage; may the world be maintained by others.' He was sharply blamed by other Rabbis." Cf. also Joh. Schneider s.v. *eùnoûchos, Theological Dictionary of the New Testament* (ed. G. Kittel, tr. G. W. Bromiley; Grand Rapids, 1964), 2, p. 767.

[14] The recent challenge to the assumption that Jesus was unmarried, William Phipps, *Was Jesus Married?* (New York, 1970), pp. 239, has not met with approval from the critics, who say that Phipps has done little more than raise the question and insinuate an affirmative answer from the practice of the culture rather than on any evidence from the gospels.

character of marriage, which his disciples are reported as comprehending in dismay (cf. Mt. 19. 10), three sayings are attributed to him that might be taken as praise for abstention from marriage. Two are eschatological, Mk. 10. 29 f. (pars. Mt. 19. 29; Lk. 18. 29b–30) and Lk. 14. 26 (par. Mt. 10. 37). Much use has been made of the first of these three texts in the Church's history of clerical celibacy. It should be quoted in its entirety:

> He said, "Not everyone can accept this teaching (*où pántes chōroûsin tòn lógon toûton*, i.e., that remarriage after divorce is adultery), only those to whom it is given to do so. Some men are incapable of sexual activity from birth (*eìsìn gàr eùnoûchoi, hoìtines 'ek koilías mētros*); some have been deliberately made so *eùnouchísthesan hypò tōnpanthrōpōn*); and some there are who have freely renounced sex for the sake of God's reign (*kaì eìsìn eùnoûchoi, hoìtines eùnoúchisan heautoùs dià tēn basileían tōn oùranōn*). Let him accept (*chōreítō*) this teaching who can." (Mt. 19. 11 f.)

The Hebrew Scriptures were thoroughly unfriendly to castration (cf. Deut. 23. 2; but also Is. 56. 4 ff.). The term *eùnoûchos* (Heb. *saris*) came to mean a man with a military commission or one in power; it did not necessarily imply emasculation. It is not to be supposed that Jesus went against Jewish teaching by favouring castration, least of all with the cultic practice of Asia Minor in mind which transformed the *eùnoûchos hiereus* into the mode of being of deity, as virginity was intended to do with women. The evangelist has him challenge the marriage customs of the time ("Let him accept this teaching who can") by holding out to some a transcendence of ordinary domesticity. There is no precise relation established between abstention from sex and the *basileía*, only the hint that the latter's demands may indicate the wisdom of the former.

The saying in Mt. 19. 11 f. is clearly cognate with the other two in the renunciatory vein (Mk. 10. 29 f. and pars.; Lk. 14. 26 and par.). In the first Jesus indicates that giving up home, brothers or sisters, mother or father, children or property, "for me and for the Gospel" is to be rewarded a hundredfold in this age and in the age to come with everlasting life. Luke's addition of "wife" (18. 29) may be an expansion but this cannot be proved; his version and that of Mk./Mt. are literarily independent. In any case, following Jesus may mean hard surrender including the sundering of family ties.

The case is the same with the second set of parallels. Luke again is alone in having "his wife" (14. 26), which may testify to the literary tradition he is following or be a conscious addition.

No case can be made for a special class to whom any one of the above sayings refers. In Mt. 19. 10 the conversation is held with "the disciples"; those who renounce sex for the sake of God's reign are "some" (*hoítines*). In Mt. 10. 37 the subject is "whoever loves" (*ho philōn*); in Lk. 14. 26 "anyone" (*tis*). Mk. 10. 29 and Lk. 18. 29 put it negatively, "no one", Mt. 19. 29 "everyone". A knowledge of the history of forms tells us not to attach any significance to Lk.'s "Peter said" (18. 28) or to identify "the disciples" of Mt. with "the Twelve". In a word, what Jesus says about "eunuchs for the sake of the kingdom" (Mt. 19. 12) he says to everyone. Response by individuals will determine to whom it is addressed. A time will come when believers will have to choose between him and family or friends.

In the resurrection logion of Mk. 12. 24 ff. (pars. Mt. 22. 29 f.; Lk. 20. 34 ff.) the first two evangelists have Jesus taking the ordinary Pharisaic view on the resurrection of the body in which the terms of life as we know it will be substantially altered. Lk. elsewhere (14. 14) seems at pains to correct the impression that might be given by the phrase "the resurrection of the dead" by speaking of "the resurrection of the just". The qualification in Lk. 20. 35, "those who have been judged worthy (*hoi dè kataxiō-théntes*) of a place in the age to come and of resurrection from the dead", is probably a divine passive characteristic of apocalyptic writing. They shall be as if unmarried (verse 35) and no longer liable to death (verse 36). Again, Jesus is reported as enunciating the ordinary Pharisaic teaching on the differences that will mark risen life in the body.

Whether Paul was a widower, had never married, or had left his wife "for the sake of God's reign" is impossible to determine.[15]

---

[15] Cf. J. Jeremias, "War Paulus Witwer?" *ZNW*, 25 (1926), pp. 310 ff.; *Nochmals: W.P.W.?* 28 (1929), pp. 321 ff., who holds that he was widowed. Ph. Ménoud inclines to the view that he was separated from his Jewish wife at the time of his conversion. Cf. "Mariage et célibat, selon saint

It is clear that his personal predilection was for the unmarried life. Paul does not find the sex life of the married defiling so much as distracting; it is a demanding human activity which can interfere with prayer, just as marriage keeps one from the things of the Lord (cf. 1 Cor. 7. 5, 32, 34). The tract *Berakoth* (ii, 5) excuses the newly married man from saying the *Shema* for the reason that Paul gives. Those who seem to be putting the question in verse 1 (many exegetes would put 1b in quotation marks) need to be reminded that it is they who put a strain on marriage by withholding "conjugal obligations" (verse 3). Paul's concession is introduced by the word "unless"; the abstention from sex is therefore the concession to the ascetically-minded Corinthians, provided there are two of them in a marriage and not just one.

The key verse for our purposes is 7: "I should like all men to be as I am myself." Barrett holds that Paul's *thelō* should here be translated not as above but "I desire", since he characteristically uses the imperfect if he has an unattainable wish in mind.[16] Paul's absolute wish for all, in this view, is chastity, not celibacy, as the next sentence will indicate: "Still, each one has his own gift from God, one this and another that" (verse 7). Paul cannot be declaring chastity and its lack to be equally gifts from God. He first wills the gift (*chárisma*) of chaste conduct for all and then distinguishes between its celibate and married forms.

Paul is obviously not praising celibacy and marriage equally, but his chief approval goes to the gift of obedience to God or restraint. While grateful for the form it takes in him, he knows that certain others may be self-deluded if they think they have the gift of celibacy. The approval Paul gives to what is probably a Corinthian proposition, "A man is better off having no relations with a woman", is sharply qualified. He fears the boast of strength in those who do not have the gift, certain married enthusiasts in the Corinthian community, and assumes that it can lead to injustice in marriage.

As to the married who subsequently come to feel that they do not need marriage, Paul charges them as from the Lord to either

---

Paul", *RThPh*, 3 ser. I (1951), pp. 21–34. Marriage appears to have been obligatory for a Jewish man. Cf. Billerbeck, II, 372.

[16] C. K. Barrett, *A Commentary on the First Epistle to the Corinthians* (New York, 1968), p. 158.

remain together or be reconciled (verses 10 f.). He wants to "promote what is good, what will help you to devote yourselves entirely to the Lord" (verse 35). Two things that can interfere with this are being "on fire" (verse 9), i.e., with unsatisfied desire, and acquiring new worries through changing one's state (verse 32). Paul is strongly persuaded that it is unwise to be "divided" (*meméristai*, verse 33) by the responsibilities of marriage. As a trustworthy counsellor, it seems good to him in the present time of stress for a person to continue as he is (cf. verse 26).

Consideration of the *'enestōsan 'anagkēn* or "present stress" seems to be the chief factor underlying Paul's conviction about remaining a slave (verse 21), a spouse (verse 27), a single person (verse 27) or a virgin (verses 25 f.; 36). One can make the case that his expectation of the shortness of the time (verse 29) governs thoroughly his thought on change of state. One can also make the case that Paul, a strong believer in marriage, has a long-held personal preference that puts it second (verses 27, 33). It is not simply that Paul's teaching would be otherwise if he were not expecting the Lord's return. It is that he appreciates his *chárisma* of "undividedness" and is strong in praise of it, quite apart from the *parousía*. But, says Paul, "With respect to virgins [the virgins of verses 36 ff.?], I have not received any commandment from the Lord" (verse 25).

As to reasons for his favouring celibacy for himself, Paul never ties it directly to his mission as an apostle. His calling may be an additional reason to be grateful for his gift but he does not make the connection. He addresses himself to the Corinthians generally, not to fellow apostles. Neither does he make a connection between marriage and the Lord's Supper in this or any extant letter.

St Paul at one point asks rhetorically whether he and Barnabas alone are without the right to "take about a Christian sister as wife (*'adelphēn gynaīka periágein*) like the rest of the apostles and the brothers of the Lord and Cephas?" (1 Cor. 9. 5). The normal behaviour of fellow apostles is perfectly right for him; he is in no secondary condition with respect to them. *Adelphē* is universally taken by commentators to signify a believer here, i.e., a Christian, and *gynē* a wife rather than any woman. The early Church fathers, as we shall see, took Paul to be describing unmarried women companions in the spreading of the Gospel. When Paul asks at the outset of this chapter, "Am I not free?" (1 Cor. 9. 1), he wants to make it clear that his curbing of his freedom out of love and service does not mean that his freedom does not exist.

As regards the bishops, deacons and elders of the epistles to Timothy and Titus (1 Tim. 3. 2, 12; Tit. 1. 6), the prospective office-holder is required in all three cases to be *miās gynaikòs anēr*. Some commentators hold that the phrase means he should be in actual fact monogamous, others that he be married but once and not successively polygamous, whether through divorce or the death of spouses. The phrase probably means exactly what it says: "a one-woman man", a husband who has a name for fidelity. That the texts do not prohibit second marriage seems clear from Paul's teaching in 1 Cor. 7. 8 f. and 39 to Christians generally, where such marriages are permitted as a matter of course.

We have in 1 Timothy 5. 11 something of the Church's later displeasure with second marriages as a breach of trust: "Refuse to enrol the younger widows, for when their passions estrange them from Christ they will want to marry." A pledge to Christ (as their spouse? Christ understood as the community?) is assumed here. The counsel given contradicts Paul's in 1 Cor. 7. 25-31, where the imminent end of the age is supposed, but it is in line with the writer's view on the goodness of everything in creation received with thanks (1 Tim. 4. 3 f.).

The theologically sophisticated author of Hebrews says nothing about a share in Christ's priesthood by a class of cultic priests. At every turn the epistle denies a common lot between him and the earthly priests operating under the law (cf. 8. 4 f.). Consequently, there are no prescriptions for the ritual holiness of Christian priests. The argument of Hebrews is one of silence and would go in the direction that while the all-sufficient priesthood of Christ makes its sharers holy in an ethical sense, any efforts of theirs at ritual purification has been rendered needless. In the epistle's sole mention of marriage there is the injunction to hold it in honour and flee fornication and adultery (13. 4).

The setting of Rev. 14. 4 on Mount Zion recalls that the Apocalyptist is exegeting Psalm 2 in a Christian sense. The 144,000 virgins (*parthénoi*) who have been previously enumerated by tribes (Rev. 7. 4–8) comprise a military roll-call like the census of 1 Chr. 4–7, and can be deduced from their long white robes and palm branches (7. 9) to be martyrs. The symbolism derives from the regulations for holy war (cf. Deut. 20; 23. 9 f.; Lev. 15. 16). This warrior-class is viewed as "the first fruits of mankind for God and the Lamb" (14. 4; cf. Ex. 24. 22; Lev. 23. 15–22; 1 Cor. 15. 20, 23; Rom. 8. 23). They have been ransomed by offering their lives to God in sacrifice as "the opening ceremony of a great harvest-home".[17] J. Jeremias speculates that the eunuch-saying of Mt. 19. 12 may have been a later development related to this passage in Revelation.[18]

Turning to the post-biblical development, we find a phrase in the letter of Ignatius to Polycarp in which the boasting of a man who lives continently (*'en agneía*) is reprobated. A faulty translation could convey the meaning: "And if he is more highly esteemed than the bishop [through his continence, i.e.], he is undone."[19] The passive of *gignōskō*, however, *gnōsthē*, is never used to signify "to be esteemed" but always "to be made known".[20] Hence, no comparison in which a married bishop is viewed unfavourably is intended.

Certain second-century texts refer to married men among the ministers of the Church, among them Polycarp's letter to the Philippians (11 : 4) and Irenaeus' *Against Heresies* (1, 13, 5). At the same time some clerics of this period like Melito, Bishop of Sardis (d. ca. 175) were choosing the celibate life and being held in honour for it.[21]

The encratite strain of thought and gnostic dualism made progress and common cause during the second half of the second century. Among those committed to encratism (*egrateía* = self-

---

[17] G. B. Caird, *A Commentary on the Revelation of St. John the Divine* (New York, 1966), p. 180.

[18] Joachim Jeremias, *New Testament Theology, The Proclamation of Jesus* (Philadelphia, 1971), p. 224.

[19] James A. Kleist, *The Epistles of St. Clement of Rome and Ignatius of Antioch*, "Ancient Christian Writers" 1 (Westminster, Md., 1946), p. 98.

[20] Thus J. B. Lightfoot and A. D'Alès as cited in Roger Gryson, *Les origines du célibat ecclésiastique* (Gembloux, 1968), pp. xi and 228.

[21] Cf. Eusebius, *The History of the Church*, 5, 24, 5: "Melito, the celibate [*eúnoûchon*], who lived entirely in the Holy Spirit." H. Leclercq thinks "celibate" a title like "bishop and martyr", art. "Célibat", *Dictionnaire d'Archéologie Chrétienne et Liturgie*, 2, 2808.

restraint) were Tatian the Syrian who rejected marriage entirely, and followed Marcion.[22] To the Pythagorean philosopher Sextus are attributed certain *Sayings*, moral sentences and rules of life which counselled against marriage.[23] Rufinus of Aquileia (d. 410) later translated them from Greek into Latin and erroneously attributed them to Pope Sixtus (d. 258), a significant confusion.

Clement of Alexandria (d. before 215) tells a tale of Nicolaos, one of the deacons of Acts 6. 5, who far from being promiscuous as the sect claimed in naming him their founder, brought his wife "into the midst of the apostles as the renunciation of desire; it was mastery of the pleasures so eagerly sought that taught him the rule 'treat the flesh with contempt'. For in obedience to the Saviour's command, I imagine, he had no wish to serve two masters, pleasure and Lord."[24] He lists against the Encratites the apostles known to have been married men, among them Peter and Philip (the latter confused with the evangelist Philip), and says that Paul does not hesitate to address his yoke-fellow, whom he did not take round with him for fear of hindering his ministry.[25]

Clement is wrong in supposing that "my dependable fellow worker" (*gnēsie sýzyge*) of Phil. 4. 3 can be Paul's wife—at least there is no textual witness for what would be the correct feminine form, *gnēsia*. He writes that if Paul lived with his wife he would disedify those who wished to live continently.[26]

How, he asks, can anyone denigrate the work of procreation if the Church is to be governed by a bishop who is "a good manager of his household", and if union "with one woman only" constitutes a home agreeable to the Lord?[27] Gryson calls Clement the one among the early Fathers who has the most positive attitude towards marriage and who does not make greater demands than Paul.[28]

The *Didascalia Apostolorum* (first half of the third century)

[22] Cf. Eusebius, 4, 29 quoting Irenaeus, *Adv. Haer.* Book I.
[23] E. T. by F. C. Conybeare, *The Ring of Pope Xystus* (London, 1910).
[24] *Miscellanies (Stromata)*, 3, 4, 25 f. Cited by Eusebius, 3, 29.
[25] *Ibid.*, 3, 6, 52 f. Quoted by Eusebius, 3, 30.
[26] *Ibid.*, 4, 15, 97.
[27] *Ibid.*, 3, 18, 108; 3, 12, 79.
[28] Gryson, *op. cit.*, p. 13.

supposes that candidates for the bishopric will be married men or widowers and stresses the criteria of Timothy for a good family man (2, 2, 2–4).

A definite change in attitude comes with the writings of Tertullian (d. after 220), Hippolytus (d. 235) and Origen (d. 253–4). All three are opposed to clerical marriage—Tertullian in his later, Montanist period to all marriage. All hint, without producing evidence, that the marriage of clergy is widespread and all intimate that laws exist prohibiting it, a claim which cannot be confirmed from any other sources. Tertullian praises the "many" in the various *ordines ecclesiastici* (bishops, presbyters, widows) who practise continence, preferring marriage with God and restoring their flesh to its pristine dignity by killing all desire.[29] Tertullian lets slip in his argument that bishops are chosen from men married once or even (*aut etiam*)—therefore the unusual case—virgins[30] Against those who would remarry he says that Paul did not marry when he might have (1 Cor. 9. 5), "thereby inviting us to follow his example".[31] The women companions of the apostles provided for their table needs but were not their wives. How could the Lord have sent the apostles abroad preaching "the sanctity of the flesh" without their providing a good example of it?[32] Tertullian cites the prohibition against admitting remarried men to the priesthood and women to the *ordo* of widow, giving as his reason: "For the altar one prepares for God must be pure."[33] He even makes up a biblical text to suit his purpose: *"Sacerdotes mei non plus nubent"*, which is nowhere to be found in Leviticus.[34] A layman should not marry a second time because it is forbidden to priests. Yet, while recalling the deposition of certain twice-married priests, Tertullian must admit that many such continue to preside over the Eucharist without shame.[35]

Hippolytus registered shock that Pope Callixtus admitted to all three clerical orders men married a second and third time.[36] Origen departs from the stance of his predecessor in the Alexandrian catechetical school, Clement, by denying any fatherhood

---

[29] *De exhortatione castitatis*, 13, 4.
[30] *Ibid.*, 11, 2.
[31] *Ibid.*, 8, 3.
[32] *De monogamia*, 8. 4–7.
[33] *Ad uxorem*, 1, 7. 4.
[34] *De exhortatione castitatis*, 7. 1.
[35] *De monogamia*, 12, 3.
[36] *Katà pasōn haireseōn*, 9, 12, 22.

to priests of the new law but a spiritual one like St. Paul's.[37]
He does not want them to beget children because he finds something impure and unseemly in sexual relations, from which
Christians, "after the manner of perfect priests", abstain totally.[38]
Those who enjoy the pleasures of love are "somehow in a state
of defilement and impurity".[39] Virgins, the once-married, and
those who persevere in chastity are "the Church of God". After
them come those who are saved by calling on Christ but who
will not be crowned by him.[40] His favourite texts are Ex. 19. 15;
1 Sam. 21. 5; and 1 Cor. 7. 5. These he uses to support his views
on sex and marriage derived from sources other than the Bible
(among them that the Logos is our hemlock, i.e., an anaphrodisiac
such as the pagan priests applied to their virile parts).[41]

Accounts of the persecutions of the latter half of the third and
early fourth century (under Decius, Diocletian and Maximinian)
bring to light numerous mentions of married bishops and priests.[42]
If the opposite tradition is as strong, nothing of this is recorded.
The abuse of clergy living with "spiritual brides" belongs to the
period, however, and is firmly reprobated.[43] Manichean doctrine
flourished during these decades and was met with by repressive
legislation from the empire. Marriage cannot be said to have risen
in esteem in Christian circles. Arnobius the Elder, an adult convert and rhetorician of Numidia, speaks of sex as *foeditas ista
coeundi*[44] and *obscenitas coeundi*.[45] The gathering of the forces of
Stoic, Pythagorean, neo-Platonic and Manichean teaching makes
understandable the famous canon 33 of the Synod of Elvira (A.D.
300 or 303) which prohibited *in totum* bishops, priests and
deacon or any clerics engaged in ministry from having their
wives or begetting sons.[46]

The phrase *"in totum"* indicates that the matter had a history
and that the partial abstention which might have been in force
must now yield to full. Another canon, 27, prescribes that while

---

[37] *Homilías perì Leuitikou*, 4. 6.
[38] *Katà Kélsou*, 7. 48.
[39] *Tómos perì Matthaiou*, 17, 35.
[40] *Homilíai perì Loukâ*, 17.
[41] Cf. n. 39, *supra*.
[42] Cf. Gryson, *op. cit.*, pp. 32–36.
[43] *Ibid.*, pp. 36–38; cf. Eusebius, *op. cit.*, 7, 30, 13.
[44] *Contra Nationes*, 4, 19.
[45] *Ibid.*, 3, 9.
[46] Denzinger–Schönmetzer, *Enchiridion Symbolorum*, 119.

the sister or virgin daughter of a bishop or other cleric may live with him, no stranger in this situation may.[47]

The chief reason alleged in favour of clerical celibacy at the turn of the fourth century was the demeaning quality of sex and its capacity for rendering impure those who engaged in it. This impurity was not moral so much as ritual in the sense of "ill-befitting", "out of character". The increasingly poor view of marriage in Christian circles was the root cause of such an outlook.[48] Isadore of Pelusium (d. ca. 435), an Egyptian monk, praised virginity because it made men to be as angels, while in marriage they differed little from animals. For him, no work of God was quite so splendid as the union in one person of priesthood and virginity. If priests deviate from chastity they lose their dignity.[49]

Eusebius of Caesarea argued that monks, because they are consecrated (*hierōmenois*) and have devoted themselves to God's service (*therapeían*), should desist from marital intercourse in the exercise of their sacred function (*hierourgían*).[50] He also proposed that teachers and preachers of the word should be "totally detached from ties and every sort of concern".[51] The patriarchs of old had their children early—*before* their great theophanies—after which they stopped.[52]

Epiphanius of Salamis made the case that the Church had always found it fitting that those who celebrated the divine cult should be distracted by nothing (*áperispástous*) so that they could fulfil their spiritual functions with a free spirit. If Paul would have even lay people be free for prayer for a time, "How much more does he prescribe the same for a priest!"[53]

Gregory of Nazianzen the young (his father was bishop of that see), himself a celibate, deplores people who avoid being baptized

---

[47] *Ibid.*, 118.

[48] Full documentation on this change is given in Bernard Lohkamp, "Cultic Purity and the Law of Celibacy", *Review for Religious*, 30 (March 1971), pp. 199–217, esp. p. 200, n. 9. Lohkamp establishes that cultic purity was the chief factor in clerical celibacy. Beginning with Pope John XXIII, utterances such as those of Pope Paul VI and Vatican Council II have been completely silent on it as a reason for the celibate life of priests.

[49] *Letters*, 3, 75. Cited by Gryson, p. 51.

[50] *Euaggelikē apódeixis*, 1, 8, 1–3.   [51] *Ibid.*, 1, 9, 14–15.

[52] *Ibid.*   [53] *Panárion*, 59, 4, 1–7.

by married priests: "That would be terrible, if I were to be defiled at the instant I was purified!"[54]

Certain fourth-century legislation allowed candidates for
deaconship to marry if they feared that out of weakness they
could not persevere. The Canons of Timothy of Alexandria ask
(c. 5) if a married couple may communicate after a night of
intercourse: "They cannot do so immediately, for the Apostle
teaches...", at which point 1 Cor. 7. 5 is quoted, with its admonition to separate for a while for prayer.[55] Canon 13 says, after
having quoted the same verse: "There must be abstinence on
Saturday and Sunday since on these days one offers spiritual
sacrifice to God."[56] Since there was no different discipline for
clergy and laity in these matters, it is evident why a married
clergy remained possible in the East where there was no daily
celebration of the Eucharist. The West with its different liturgical practice came to have a different discipline.

The Western development was influenced chiefly by fourth-
and fifth-century popes and theologians like Damasus, Siricius,
Jerome and Ambrosiaster. They do not allege any new reasons
or use biblical texts in any new way, except perhaps in their care-
less accommodation of texts like, "But you are not in the flesh,
you are in the spirit" (Rom. 8. 9), to apply to clergy.

The decretal of Pope Damasus to the bishops of Gaul, in response to some questions they put, conveys the whole mentality
of the age. After a tissue of texts which includes 1 Cor. 7. 29,
Rom. 13. 14 and 1 Cor. 7. 7, there is cited the presumed practice
of the priests of Israel whereby they lived for a year within the
temple precincts in order to be pure, disregarding their families
throughout. (Subsequent popes repeat this error, the origin of
which is unknown.) Idolaters who "practised their impious cult
and offered immolation to demons" imposed on themselves continence with regard to women and abstention from certain
goods.[57] "Those who put themselves in the service of creatures in

<hr/>

[54] *Lógos*, 4, 26.
[55] *Joannou*, 2, 242 f. Cited by Gryson, p. 123.
[56] *Joannou*, 248 f.
[57] "These Oriental religions pretended to restore lost purity.... Their
rites were supposed to regenerate the initiated person and restore him to
an immaculate and incorruptible life.... Abstinence, which prevented the
introduction of deadly elements into the system, and chastity, which pre-

performing the work of generation may well bear the name of priest but they are not worthy of it. . . . The mystery of God may not be entrusted to men like this, 'defiled unbelievers' (Tit. 1. 15), in whom the holiness of the body is polluted by impurity and incontinence . . . yet the priest or deacon dares to lower himself and become like the animals."[58] Pope Damasus is likewise the author of the sentiment, *"Commixtio pollutio est"* ("Intercourse is defilement"). The theme of ritual cleanliness found frequent expression in that epoch, during which the offices of bishop, presbyter and deacon were being given the entire cultural baggage of Roman and Israelite priesthood and sacrifice.

The conclusion pointed to by the data above is that clerical celibacy developed in both East (as partial) and West (as total) as the expression of a view within the Church unsympathetic to sex and marriage. The development was largely independent of the biblical data on the subject. Rather, there was a general suspicion of the marriage act as defiling, which was made to centre on the leaders of cult. To have extended the view to all the married would have opened the Church to the charge of gnostic dualism. The Church remained biblically oriented in appearance, although not in fact, by exegeting incorrectly a number of Pauline references to marriage and abstention, and by identifying "flesh" (*sarx*)—which in the New Testament means resistance to God's spirit (*pneuma*)—with the marriage act.

---

served man from pollution and debility, became means of getting rid of the domination of the evil powers and of regaining heavenly favour." Franz Cumont, *Oriental Religions in Roman Paganism* (New York, 1956), pp. 39 f. (orig. ed. 1911); cf. E. Fehrle, *Die kultische Keuschheit im Altertum* (Giessen, 1910).

[58] Pope Damasus, *Decretal to the Bishops of Gaul*, 2, 5-6. Quoted in Gryson, pp. 129 ff.

Demetrios Constantelos

Marriage and Celibacy of the Clergy in the Orthodox Church

IN THE Orthodox Church there are married and unmarried clergymen. Most presbyters and deacons are married, while all bishops
are celibate—save a few who are widowers.

The Orthodox Church today favours and practises optional
celibacy. But canon law rules, and the practice is that the individual who plans to enter the priesthood must decide before
ordination whether he desires to serve the Church as a married
man or as a celibate. Once a decision is made, the individual
is expected to honour it and to stay in the status he chose. No
marriage is permitted after ordination, and no second marriage
is allowed for a priest who has lost a wife either through death or
by divorce. Widowers who are elected to the episcopal office
usually have no children, or their children are adults.

What are the theological presuppositions which have served the
development of this practice in Orthodoxy? The answer is that
the Church sees both marriage and virginity (which is identified
with celibacy—celibacy without virginity and a pure life is un-
thinkable, at least in theory) as holy states. Marriage is a mystery
of the Church; it is an honourable sacrament through which God
himself perpetuates his creative and evolutionary work through
the mutual consent, love and union of two individuals of opposite
sexes, who serve as his co-workers in creation. Marriage is not a
contract, but a sacred and creative function, consummation of
two persons into a twofold being—a new Adam.

While marriage is honoured as a natural, God-given institution,
virginity or celibacy is viewed as a state above nature, a special

gift from God bestowed on a few. Thus, "not all men receive it, but they to whom it is given. . . . He who is able to receive this call [to celibacy], let him receive it" (Mt. 19. 10–12). If a candidate for the priesthood is not certain of his call to serve God and the Church as a celibate, if he has even slight doubts about his ability to remain a virgin, he is advised by his counsellor and spiritual father to marry.

Orthodox theologians emphasize that the Church has applied to the question of marriage and celibacy the principle of moderation, the measure (to metron), and discretion (diakrisis), respect for personal decision. The Church has practised this principle of option and free will for many centuries. In fact, the Orthodox believe that their faith and practice in this area correspond to the faith and practice of the Apostolic Church.

In the Apostolic Church there were married and unmarried clergymen, deacons (1 Tim. 3. 12) as well as priests and bishops (Tit. 1. 5–6, 1 Tim. 3. 2, 4–5). There were married and celibate Apostles. Among the twelve, only John seems to have been single, and after him St Paul. There was no distinction between married and unmarried Apostles. St Paul's advice that people remain single as he had been can be explained on the basis of his eschatological expectations. But St Paul did not condemn marriage, nor did he force anyone to stay celibate. He merely expressed an opinion, which was not binding upon the Christian community and found few devoted followers.

In the great controversies between the Apostolic Church and the Gnostic sects concerning the morality of marriage and the value of celibacy, the Church eventually adopted a position which may be described as moderate in full agreement with the Bible, socially pragmatic and realistic for human nature. While the Church praised and honoured virginity all along, it also elevated the natural state of physical union to a sacramental state. Marriage became one of the seven mysteries of the Church in which God's grace is called upon husband and wife, making them synergous, or collaborators of God in his creative work.

By the middle of the fourth century there were married and unmarried deacons, presbyters and bishops. Neither the strict Montanists nor the perverted and sensuous polygamists prevailed. The Church respected the individual's judgment with the exception that certain concrete canons were formulated to regulate the number of marriages and the time for performance of the ceremony.

It is historically true that attempts were made to impose celibacy upon all the clergy, but they failed in the Eastern Church. The first serious attempt was made in the First Ecumenical Synod in 325 by Hosius, the bishop of Cordoba, and certain other bishops from Greece proper. But their views did not prevail. The ecclesiastical historian Socrates relates that: "It seemed fit to the bishops to introduce a new law into the Church, that those who were in holy orders, I speak of bishops, presbyters, and deacons, should have no conjugal intercourse with the wives whom they had married while still laymen.... When discussion on this matter was impending, Paphnutius [Bishop of the cities in Upper Thebes in Egypt] having arisen in the midst of the assembly of bishops, earnestly entreated them not to impose so heavy a yoke on the ministers of religion: asserting that 'marriage itself is honourable, and the bed undefiled', urging before God that they ought not to injure the Church by too stringent restrictions. 'For all men,' said he, 'cannot bear the practice of rig'd continence';... and he termed the intercourse of a man with his lawful wife chastity.... The whole assembly of the clergy assented to the reasoning of Paphnutius, wherefore they silenced all further debate on this point, leaving it to the discretion of those who were husbands to exercise abstinence if they so wished in reference to their wives." Sozomenus, the other important ecclesiastical historian of the fifth century, also reports that the Fathers of the First Ecumenical Synod "enacted no law about it, but left the matter to the decision of individual judgment and not to compulsion".[1] Gelasius of Kyzikos (†ca. 475) adds that Paphnutius considered obligatory celibacy as an *hyperbole* or excessive imposition, which went beyond the demands of human nature. Hyperbolic zeal in issuing canons forbidding married bishops, priests, deacons and subdeacons to continue living with their wives, or imposing celibacy upon the new clergy can possibly hurt rather than serve the Church. "Not all can sustain the heavy burden of exercising the

[1] Socrates, *Ecclesiastical History*, I.xi; Sozomenus, *Ecclesiastical History*, I.xxiii.

mortification of natural desires."[2] Commenting on the decision of the First Ecumenical Synod, Gelasius writes that optional celibacy was adopted for the benefit of the Church.[3]

This spirit has been expressed again and again in the moral and canonical teaching of the Church. For example, the twenty-first canon of the Synod in Gangra (365) states the following: "We do, assuredly, admire virginity (celibacy) accompanied by humility; and we have regard for continence, accompanied by godliness and gravity...but at the same time we honour the holy companionship of marriage." The same council, whose canons were accepted and codified by the ecumenical synods, anathematized those who condemned marriage (such as the Gnostics) and anyone who hesitated to receive Communion from a married priest (Canon I).

Marriage of the clergy was not recommended after ordination and special canons made this a tradition. For example, the first canon of Neocaesarea (314) forbade the marriage of presbyters after ordination. The fifteenth canon of the Fourth Ecumenical Council forbade the marriage of deaconesses after their tonsure. The fourth canon of the Synod in Trullo forbade marriage after ordination for all ranks of the priesthood. Despite these restrictions, however, there were deacons and presbyters who married after ordination. This custom, though, was once again attacked in the tenth century by imperial legislation.

Until the first quarter of the sixth century, there was no discrimination against married bishops and no distinction between married and unmarried candidates for the episcopate. In fact, there were canons protecting married bishops. For example, the fifth Apostolic canon states that any bishop (or presbyter or deacon) who dismisses his wife on account of piety [or on the pretension of piety] be defrocked or even excommunicated if he insists on doing so.[4]

It is a well-known fact that there were many married bishops in the early and the medieval Eastern Church. Gregory of Nyssa, Gregory the Elder of Nazianzus, Kyros of Kotyaion, Gregory the

---

[2] Gelasius of Kyzikos, "Historia Concilii Nicaeni", XXXII MPG, vol. 85, cols. 1336–1337.
[3] *Ibid.*, col. 1337A.
[4] H. Alivizatos, *Hoi Hieroi Kanones* (Athens), p. 138.

Illuminator (or Fotistes) as well as his successors to the Catholicate of Armenia were married bishops. Synesius, another married bishop, may serve as an illustration of how the early Church respected both personal views and decisions. When elected bishop and before his ordination, Synesius made it clear that his superiors, as well as the Church as a whole, should respect his wife whom he did not intend to send to a monastery, a request which was honoured.[5]

In the Eastern Church, it was not rare for married bishops to be elevated to the Ecumenical throne. For example, Manuel I, Patriarch of Constantinople in exile at Nicaea (1217–1222), had been a married man.[6] Not only were there married priests and bishops, but there were clergymen who had married two and even three times. In the early Church, one of the controversies between bishop Callistus of Rome and the future bishop Hippolytus concerned the moral quality of the clergy. Hippolytus accused Pope Callistus of allowing digamous bishops, priests and deacons to retain their place among the clergy under his administration. Despite the injustice and the unfairness of Hippolytus towards Callistus, there is no reason to doubt his testimony that there were men who had been admitted to holy orders, even though they had married more than once.[7] Jerome confirmed that even in the Western Church, there were clergy who married after ordination. The Council of Elvira decreed that a repetition of matrimony was to be forbidden for the clergy and that any man twice married was to be excluded from holy orders. Nevertheless, married bishops attended the Synod of Rimini as well as other councils.[8] Thus, in both the East and the West, the Church was flexible and there were married clergymen in all ranks.

However, under the influence of the increasingly powerful monastic world, and that of the emperor Justinian, attempts were made in the sixth century to degrade the married presbytery and to elect all bishops from monastic communities. The philosophy

[5] Synesius of Cyrene, "Epistles", No. 105, MPG 66:1485.
[6] George Acropolites, *Annales*, 51.
[7] Hippolytus, "The Refutation of All Heresies", IX.7, *The Ante-Nicene Fathers*, vol. 5 (Grand Rapids, 1957), p. 131, col. 1.
[8] Jerome, "Epistle No. NXIX Ad Oceanum", MPL, vol. 22, cols. 653–64.

behind this legislation was that a bishop should have no family of his own because he was the father of all his flock.[9]

Nevertheless, there was a provision for the election of a married priest to the episcopate. Through his sixth decree (novel), Justinian ordered that if there was a need for the Church to ordain a bishop from the married clergy, the Church should prefer those presbyters with no children. This implies that the finances of the Church were a factor in the preference of the unmarried over the married clergy since the bishop was in charge of finances and abuses were more likely if he had to feed a family.[10]

The celibate episcopate prevailed after the Synod in Trullo (691–692), not only because of the increasing influence of monastic ideals, but as a reaction against nepotism, which tended to create problems within the Church. But there was no theological argument against a married episcopate. Notwithstanding the practical advantages of a celibate episcopate, marriage was viewed as an honourable state for all three priestly ranks (see the 51st Apostolic canon). As late as the twelfth century, there were married bishops (married laymen, who, upon ordination, had refused to send their wives to convents as had been prescribed by the Council of Trullo, canons 12 and 48). Emperor Isaac Angelus (1185–1195, 1203–1204) issued a law against this practice.[11] In the Eastern Church, celibacy was never considered an obligatory prerequisite for the priesthood in any one of the priestly ranks. The canons did not impose upon or violate the free choice of the candidate for the priesthood.

The Church sees marriage as a blessed necessity, not only from a sociological or biological point of view, but from an ethical one as well. Husband and wife are believers whose ultimate goal is to reach perfection and to inherit God's kingdom. What is very difficult for the lonely individual becomes possible for two people whose daily concern is to help each other to a satisfactory life here on earth, and also to a common victory over evil. Some see celibacy as the ultimate way to moral perfection; others believe that far from hindering the attainment of Christian virtue, mar-

[9] Justinian, *Codex*, Bk. 1.3.41 (42), sect. 1–4; 1.3.47 (48), ed. Paulus Krueger, *Corpus Juris Civilis*, vol. 2 (Berlin, 1915), pp. 26, 34.

[10] Cf. 41, Apostolic Canon.

[11] Rhollis and Potles, *Syntagma tōn Theiōn kai Hierōn Kanonōn*, vol. 2, p. 421; vol. 5, pp. 321-3.

riage is much more admirable because it implies the sharing of pain and labour, and an unselfish concern for the upbringing of children.

The majority of Orthodox theologians favour this second view. Thus, Theodore Metochites, the fourteenth-century Christian humanist and intellectual, viewed the monastic or eremitic and speculative life as a kind of escapism. Marriage, procreation of children, social involvement and action in public affairs provide greater opportunities for the realization of the Christian ideal.[12]

In order to appreciate a married clergy, we must first understand and appreciate the holiness of marriage. Those Church Fathers who exalted virginity and stressed celibacy viewed the sexual union as an act of defilement to the human soul. But the sexual act in marriage is the culmination and the supreme expression of love between husband and wife which leads them to this consummation. Furthermore, emphasis on celibacy hides inherently and subconsciously the patriarchal concept which degrades woman into a secondary position or sees her as the means through which sin was introduced in the world.

Whatever the case, it is true that the conscience of the Church or the totality of the kingdom's membership by honouring celibacy did not degrade marriage, because Christianity had already liberated and had given a new and prominent position to woman. Since in every marriage we have a re-creation of mankind or co-workers of God, a married priest is twice a co-worker of the Creator. It is interesting to note that while marriage has been elevated by the Church into a sacramental state, and is considered one of the seven mysteries, celibacy has not received a sacramental state.

Orthodox theologians advocate optional celibacy for theological reasons. But, in addition, they prefer parish priests to be married as a means of preventing moral failures and scandals in the Church, even though they realize that marriage does not necessarily solve the sexual problem. It is not unknown for married priests to violate the moral code, and the danger of preoccupying themselves with family concerns is not absent from their lives. But when the advantages and the disadvantages of married clergy

---

[12] Theodore Metochites, *Miscellanea*, ed. Muller and Kiessling, pp. 370–7.

are weighed, the advantages far outweigh the disadvantages. The married priest who has learned responsibility and awareness of his obligations may prove to be much more effective in his ministry. The celibate who confronts the world timidly, who is inexperienced in family matters, economic strains and the rearing of children; the priest who has not spent an evening at the bed of a sick child or wife, cannot possibly understand the pains and agonies of his flock. To speak *ex cathedra*, to deliver moral sermons from a pulpit distant from the problems of his people is not equal to the mellow, mature, sympathetic and understanding attitude of the family priest.

The question of a married clergy, including bishops, has been discussed repeatedly since the twelfth century, and has assumed great importance in the twentieth. Marriage after ordination, second marriages for widowed priests and married bishops, are themes of great concern to the Church today. Since marriage and ordination are sacraments of the Church, and since the marriage of the clergy is not a matter of doctrine, theologians today believe that the Church could and should make changes relevant to contemporary needs. Any change to allow marriage after ordination, a second marriage for a widowed priest or a married bishop, would be in full accord with the faith and practice of the Church in Apostolic times and in the first seven centuries of our era. Action upon these issues rests not, however, with individual hierarchs or theologians, but with the whole Orthodox Church convened in an ecumenical or pan-Orthodox Synod. Among leading churchmen in the Orthodox Church today who have favoured optional celibacy and the elevation of married priests to the episcopacy as well as marriage after ordination, we may mention the late Patriarch Athenagoras and Archbishop Iakovos of North and South America.

A heated discussion concerning a second marriage for priests and deacons in the Orthodox Church was conducted in the 1920s. The dialogue was initiated by the Church of Serbia which was faced with many widowed priests in the districts of Karlovitsi, Bukovina and Dalmatia. The Serbian Church appealed to the Ecumenical Patriarch who asked several theologians, clergymen and laymen alike, for their theological opinion. Several theological essays and views were published in the periodicals *Gregorios o*

Palamas, vols. 2, 3; *Ekklesiastikos Kyrex*, vol. 8; *Ekklesiastikos Pharos*, vol. 1; *Ekklesiastike Aletheia*, vol. 33, and others. The consensus was that a second marriage for widowed priests was both doctrinally and ethically in order. Gennadios of Thessalonike in particular, Philaretos Vafeides and Chrysanthos of Trepizond stressed the sacred aspect of marriage and encouraged the Orthodox Church to take a positive step in resolving the problem in favour of a second marriage. Unfortunately, the issue has remained under discussion to the present day.

Are the Orthodox pleased with their present system? There are several leading bishops and theologians who believe that, in addition to the above, two more changes must take place. First, marriage should be allowed after ordination. Young theological school or seminary graduates who qualify to be ordained postpone their entrance into the priesthood because they have not been able to find the appropriate spouse. Since marriage had never been an obstacle for ordination in the ancient Church, these theologians believe that marriage after ordination is desirable theologically, canonically and pragmatically. The Church will gain rather than lose.

The second change concerns the episcopate. There are Orthodox theologians who advocate the election of married priests to the rank of bishop. Theological training and other qualifications are not the exclusive possession of celibate clergy. In fact, because the Orthodox Church has fewer and fewer qualified celibate priests, the belief is that the Church must recruit its bishops from the married priests (not simply widowers).

While the first issue may be solved much more easily in a pan-Orthodox synod, the second one will encounter serious obstacles because there are still many conservative bishops in the Orthodox Church at large. Nevertheless, there is a widespread realization that the Church must squarely face the problem posed by a shortage of clergy and a shortage of celibate priests for the episcopate. Perhaps under the pressure of the needs within the Church of the 1970s, we may be forced to rediscover the faith and practice of the Apostolic Church which accorded with the Bible and respected the judgment and free will of the individual. To do so would make marriage and celibacy before or after ordination optional.

Steven Ozment

Marriage and the Ministry in the Protestant Churches

> The Lord God has wanted three things made right
> again before the last day: *Ministerium verbi, magis-*
> *tratum et coniugium.*[1]

THE Protestant concept of clerical marriage developed in opposition to priestly celibacy and monasticism. The reformers set
out to demonstrate not only in theological but in personal and
social terms the superiority of a married to a celibate clergy.
Thought and deed are truly intertwined. All the "Wittenberg
theologians" married by 1525, Luther's union with Katherine
von Bora on 13 June of that year being the last if not the least. It is
significant that in terms both of its founding (1502) and of the
ages of its professors, Wittenberg was one of the youngest German universities. In 1521, Luther at thirty-eight was among the
oldest. His co-workers were in their twenties and thirties, men
capable of being immediately touched by the issue of celibacy.[2]
Although a truly celibate life was still recognized as a rare exception (perhaps one in a thousand, Luther reckoned), the reformers concluded that marriage and family life, not celibacy and
the monastery, formed the most effective arena of Christian perfection. Accolades and values previously reserved for the solitary
life were fatefully transferred to the home. Convinced they had

---

[1] Martin Luther, *Tabletalk* No. 433 (1532), *Luthers Werke in Auswahl*
8, ed. by Otto Clemen (Berlin, 1950), p. 53.
[2] Cf. A. Franzen, *Zölibat und Priesterehe in der Auseinandersetzung*
der Reformationszeit und der katholischen Reform des 16. Jahrhunderts
(Münster, 1969), p. 30.

not only the authority of their own experience under vows, but also Scripture and tradition on their side, the reformers proceeded boldly. Luther spoke for generations of Protestant apologists when he concluded the preface to Steffan Klingebeyl's *Von Priester Ehe* (Wittenberg, 1528):

> On our side we have Scripture, the Church Fathers, ancient Church laws and even papal precedent. We'll stick to that. They have the contrary statements of a few Fathers, recent canons and their own mischief, without any support from Scripture and the Word of God. We'll let them have that.[3]

I. THE BURDEN OF CELIBACY

In the Reformation treatises of 1520, Luther urged marriage upon that "wretched multitude of priests who now sit in shame and heaviness of conscience" and declared baptism the sole and all-sufficient Christian vow.[4] But it was not Luther who authored the first incisive Protestant assault on celibacy. Andreas Boden-stein von Karlstadt (†1541) receives this honour for his *De Coelibatu, monachatu et viduitate* (Wittenberg, June 1521). A highly partisan work by a most outspoken author, it was to shape basic Protestant attitudes. Luther's own order of Augus-tinian hermits in Wittenberg embraced it enthusiastically.

To Karlstadt's mind, papal desire to increase the wealth of the Church and control over the clergy lay at the root of celibacy. A seed bed of sexual perversion and crime, the celibate life was seen to encourage homosexuality and that greatest of all sexual transgressions, masturbation—the giving of one's seed to Moloch.[5]

---

[3] B 1 a (copy in Yale's Beineke Library) (= *WA* 26, 533.26–31).

[4] *An Open Letter to the Christian Nobility of the German Nation* in *Three Treatises: Martin Luther* (Philadelphia, 1960), pp. 67 f. (= *WA* 6, pp. 440–3); *The Babylonian Captivity of the Church*, in *ibid.*, pp. 198 f. (= *WA* 6, 538.26–9). In the *Dictata super Psalterium* (1513–1516) and the *Lectures on Romans* (1515–1516), *fides*, not chastity, is the antidote to concupiscence, and the ideal of Christian community is critically juxtaposed to the "separatism" of monks. B. Lohse, *Mönchtum und Reformation: Luthers Auseinandersetzung mit dem Mönchsideal des Mittelalters* (Göttingen, 1963), esp. pp. 236–41, 269. The key to the final break with celibate vows lay in the growing conviction that baptismal vows were absolutely final for the Christian. *Ibid.*, pp. 278, 333, 351–2.

[5] A 4 b (copy in Yale's Beineke Library). Karlstadt's views are discussed

It was an ideal designed to promote fornication and guilt, which could in turn be absolved for an appropriate fee.[6]

Karlstadt drew seven conclusions in opposition. First, the period of probation for the religious should be extended to cover the full duration of sexual desire and titillation; at age sixty, one might reasonably be expected to fulfil celibate vows. Until then nuns can best be "living temples" by motherhood. "It is better to make a home and teach the Word of God to one's family than to mutter frigid prayers in a sanctuary." Domestic life and labour in the secular world are *"honestius"*.[7] Secondly, only those who have been married are qualified to enter holy orders (a conclusion Karlstadt extracted from 1 Tim. 3. 2).[8] Thirdly, if any in religious orders burn with desire, they can and should marry.[9] Fourthly, since vows are valid only when the one vowed to reciprocates (Num. 30. 12), the vow of celibacy remains invalid and unfulfilled until it is known whether God approves it. Karlstadt maintained that indications of divine approval are most likely to appear after age sixty.[10] Fifthly, the incontinence of those under vows is a far greater evil than the lust of a husband for his wife, and, judged by their fruits, marriage is a far greater good than celibacy. "Marriage produces children, rears them in the faith, makes men of them, cultivates the earth, and is vigilant in charity. Celibacy very often destroys boys and makes deserts of the earth."[11] Sixthly, priests desiring marriage can break their vows without sin, since such have been based on a false understanding of human nature. "Roman pontiffs, ignorant of Holy Scripture, have never understood the force of human weakness."[12] Finally, inasmuch as marriage is the only effective cure for fornication, Karlstadt would have bishops force priests living in concubinage to marry[13]—a suggestion enacted as law when Protestants rewrote the marriage ordinances of their regions.

Luther's reaction to Karlstadt's views was mixed. He puzzled over some of his scriptural interpretations, but empathized with

---

in larger context by H. Barge, *Andreas Bodenstein von Karlstadt* I (Leipzig, 1905), pp. 265 ff.

[6] A 3 a.

[7] B 3 b; C 2 a–C 4 a. The age limit of sixty is taken from 1 Tim. 5. 9.

[8] C 4 a.   [9] D 2 a–b.

[10] D 3 a.   [11] D 3 b.

[12] D 4 a.   [13] D 4 b.

the "wretched men, boys and girls vexed with pollutions and burnings".[14] He could not, however, simply equate the freely elected vows of monks with those imposed upon priests.[15] Although distrusting his hesitation ("I don't know what phantom of pomp and human opinion is plaguing me here") and even convinced that chastity should not be "voked",[16] he was still able to assure Spalatin in August 1521: "Good Lord! Will our people at Wittenberg give wives even to monks? They will not push a wife on me!"[17]

Luther soon capitulated to the logic of his convictions, as the appearance of the *De Votis monasticis iudicium* (later 1521) and *Vom Ehelichen Leben* (1522) testify. The former set forth the magisterial Protestant case against celibate vows. It argued that vows lack scriptural authority and oppose faith, evangelical freedom, the commandment to love one's neighbour, and common sense and reason. In the Bible, Luther maintained, Christ discouraged rather than counselled celibacy, having dealt with it approvingly only in a passing statement on eunuchs. And Paul discussed it as an "open matter", not as a direct invitation. "A *vow* of chastity ... is diametrically opposed to the Gospel."[18]

Vows oppose faith, Luther argued, because they spurn the grace of baptism, looking down upon the acceptance of God's promise in the baptismal vow as but a penultimate step. This assumption of religious superiority led Luther finally to release monks also from their vows.

The idea of a voluntary vow not imposed upon them by someone else has strongly influenced me until now. But it influences me no longer.... They teach justification and salvation by works, and depart from faith. They not only think that their obedience, poverty and chastity are certain roads to salvation, but that their ways are more perfect and better than those of the rest of the faithful.[19]

[14] Letter to Melanchthon (1 Aug. 1521) in *Luther's Works* 48, p. 279 (= *WABr* 2, 371, pp. 47-50).
[15] *Ibid.*, p. 277 (= *WABr* 2, pp. 370 ff).
[16] Letter to Melanchthon (3 Aug. 1521) in *ibid.*, pp. 287, 285 (= *WABr* 2, pp. 374-5).
[17] Letter to Spalatin (6 Aug. 1521) in *ibid.*, p. 290 (= *WABr* 2, 377.4-6).
[18] *Luther's Works* 44, 262 (= *WA* 8, 584.8-9).
[19] *Ibid.*, p. 285 (= *WA* 8, 589.12-16). The flagellant movement, which

Luther considered vows to be in opposition to Christian liberty because they infringed upon the "pact of freedom" which God made with Christians in baptism. According to this pact, the Christian is bound only to what ensures freedom of conscience. "The freedom of the Gospel may still be retained by observing these things (poverty, obedience and chastity), but as soon as you teach them, vow them, and demand them, evangelical freedom is lost."[20]

Vows were said to transgress the commandment to love one's neighbour because they encourage a "narrow and artificial love ... preventing service to any but fellow monks".[21] And they were thought to be in contradiction with common sense and reason because they ignore the nature of man. He who is sincerely celibate today may not be able to remain so tomorrow. Echoing Karlstadt, Luther suggested the confinement of celibate vows to sixty years and older for women and "seventy or eighty" for men.[22] And, comparing the breaking of the vow of chastity when one "burns" to stealing when one faces starvation, he appealed to the honoured legal principle of *epikeia*.[23]

Luther's writings had a tremendous impact. In November 1521, fifteen left the Augustinian cloister in Wittenberg, the beginning of an apparent mass exodus from the ranks of German Augustinians. From the cloister key figures entered both the work of the Reformation and the estate of marriage. From the Augustinians came Wenzeslaus Linck, Johann Lang and Gabriel Zwilling; from the Franciscans, Eberlin of Günzburg, Konrad Pellikan, Franz Lambert of Avignon and Friedrich Myconius;

---

came to a peak in 1349, also described itself as a "second baptism", superior to sacramental baptism. Cf. G. Leef, *Heresy in the Later Middle Ages* II (Manchester, 1967), p. 489.

[20] *Luther's Works* 44, p. 315 (= *WA* 8, 616.26–31).

[21] *Ibid.*, p. 335 (= *WA* 8, 628.28–33). The *Confessio Tetrapolitana* censured monastic vows for suspending man's first social duty: the love and service of his neighbour. B. Moeller, *Reichstadt und Reformation* (Gütersloh, 1962), p. 46, n. 63. Moeller makes too much of the distinction between Luther's theologically oriented and Bucer's socially directed first line of defence against vows. Cf. H. J. Grimm, "Luther's Contributions to 16th Century Organization of Poor Relief", *ARG* 61 (1970), pp. 222–34.

[22] *Luther's Works* 44, pp. 360, 387 ff., 398 (= *WA* 8, 644.15 ff., 661.8 ff., 667.34 ff.).

[23] *Ibid.*, p. 391 (= *WA* 8, 663.23 ff.; cf. 664.21–22).

from the Dominicans, Martin Bucer; and from the Benedictines, Ambrosius Blarer. Johann Bugenhagen, Justus Jonas, Georg Spalatin, Nicholas of Amsdorf, Urbanus Rhegius and Johann Oecolampadius stepped forth from the ranks of the secular clergy.[24]

As was fitting in the sixteenth century, before political replaced religious ideologies, Karlstadt and Luther stressed biblical and theological arguments against the vow of celibacy. But the existential rootage of these arguments should not go unobserved. In their experience they found the celibate life an intolerable personal and vocational burden, a tyrannical ideal, a *"non casta castitas"*, as Justus Jonas put it.[25] Though often articulated more bluntly, this experience was fully shared by the Reformed and Anglican communities. Especially revealing is the petition in July 1522 by eleven prominent Swiss clergy to the bishop of Constance, bearing the title: *Petition of Certain Preachers of Switzerland to the Most Reverend Lord Hugo, Bishop of Constance, That He Will Not Suffer Himself to be Persuaded to Make Any Proclamation to the Injury of the Gospel, nor Endure Longer the Scandal of Harlotry, but Allow the Priests to Marry Wives or at Least Would Wink at Their Marriages.* These clergy were led by Ulrich Zwingli, who was at the time secretly married to a widow, Anna Reinhart.

According to the petition, the present situation, with clergy everywhere covertly maintaining unlawful wives, was a detriment to the ministry: "How ... will the simple-minded common man believe in him who even while he preaches the Gospel is thought by them to be licentious and a shameless dog? Can anything happen more disastrous to our sacred calling?"[26] Chastity, a matter more easily legislated than maintained, has caused these men to fear for their very sanity.

[24] Franzen, *op. cit.*, p. 29.

[25] *Adversus Iohannem Fabrum Constantienem Vicarium, scortationis patronum, pro coniugio sacerdotali, Iusti Ionae defensio* (Wittenberg, 1523), B 4 a (copy in Yale's Beineke Library).

[26] *The Latin Works and the Correspondence of Huldreich Zwingli* I, ed. S. M. Jackson (New York, 1912), p. 155 (= *Supplicatio (sic) quorundam apud Helvetios evangelistarum* in *Huldreich Zwinglis Sämtliche Werke*, ed. by E. Egli, I, pp. 197–209. See also *Manifestations of Discontent in Germany on the Eve of the Reformation*, ed. and trans. Gerald Strauss (Bloomington, Ind., 1971), p. 61.

While we willingly yield this glory to those who live chastely, we are grieved that it has been denied unto us. . . . We have been so on fire from passion—with shame let it be said—that we have done many things unseemly, yet whether this should not be laid upon those to some extent who have forbidden marriage we refrain from saying now, thinking it enough that the fire of passion alone (and that so frequent and violent as to threaten the mind) is pronounced sufficient reason for marriage.[27]

The petition concluded with a prophecy of the inevitability of clerical marriage:

We presage that things are going to put on a new face whether we will or no. . . . There is a report that most of the ecclesiastics have already chosen wives, not only among our Swiss, but among all peoples everywhere, and to put this down will certainly be not only beyond your strength but beyond that of one far more mighty, if you will pardon our saying so.[28]

To a significant extent, the end of clerical celibacy in Zürich climaxed rather than introduced clerical marriage. The same might be said of legislation passed in England during the reign of Edward VI. "Contemporaries did not look upon it so much in the light of a reform as of a kind of legitimizing of women hitherto in an ambiguous position."[29] Zwingli was "publicly" married in April 1524, shortly before the arrival of a child. The new marriage ordinance promulgated in Zürich in May 1525 and enforced on the surrounding villages in June 1526, gave pastors living in concubinage fourteen days either to sever the relationship or be publicly declared married.[30] Given the example of their

[27] *The Latin Works and the Correspondence of Huldreich Zwingli* I, p. 160.
[28] *Ibid.*, p. 164.
[29] J. Gairdner, *Lollardy and the Reformation in England*, III, pp. 57 f.— cited by P. Hughes, *The Reformation in England*, II (New York, 1963³), p. 115.
[30] O. Farner, *Zwingli the Reformer: His Life and Work*, trans. by D. G. Sear (1968), pp. 88-9; *Huldrych Zwingli: Seine Verkündigung und ihre ersten Früchte, 1520-1525* (Zürich, 1954), pp. 500 f. Cf. C. W. Köhler, *Zürcher Ehegericht und Genfer Konsistorium* I (Leipzig, 1932).

leaders and the push of the law, the marriage of incontinent clergy did indeed become inevitable in Zürich.

The moral urgency of the Zürich petition was echoed by John Calvin in a treatise written for Charles V in anticipation of the Diet of Speier (February 1544), *On the Necessity of Reforming the Church*.[31] In the Anglican community, the anonymous *Defence of Priestes Mariages*, written in the perilous times of the Marian persecutions, and ascribed to the archbishop of Canterbury, Matthew Parker (†1575), protested the "pretendying Chastitie" of Rome, which Mary was forcibly reinstating, as "the verie high waie to unspeakeable whoredomes and filthinesse".[32]

II. New Joys and Tribulations

If celibacy was a burden, then marriage was a boon to the ministry, according to the Protestant apologists. Jeremy Taylor, the "Shakespeare" of the Anglican divines, said it with exceptional vividness:

Celibacy, like an insect in the heart of an apple, dwells in solitude: but marriage, like the useful bee, builds a house, gathers sweetness from every flower, labours, forms societies, sends out colonies, feeds the world with delicacies, obeys the sovereign, keeps order, exercises many virtues, promotes the interest of mankind, and is that state of good things to which God hath designed the present constitution of the world.[33]

Two practical advantages of marriage were repeatedly stressed: it gave the minister an existential point of contact with his parishioners, and it stabilized the personal life of the majority of clerics who were incapable of chastity.

---

[31] *Calvin: Theological Treatises* (Philadelphia, 1954), p. 215 (= *Supplex exhortatio ad Caesarem Carolum V et Principes aliosque ordines Spirae nunc imperii conventum agentes, ut restituendae ecclesiae curam serio velint suscipere*, CR 34, 498). Calvin's criticism of monasticism is traced by F. Biot, *The Rise of Protestant Monasticism* (Baltimore, 1963), pp. 29–46.

[32] *A Defence of Priestes Mariages, Stablysshed by the Imperial Lawes of the Realme of England, Against a Civilian Naming Hymselfe Thomas Martin, Doctour of the Civile Lawes* (London, 1567?), 2 b (copy in Yale's Beineke Library).

[33] *The Marriage Ring; or, The Mysteriousness and Duties of Marriage* (Birmingham, 1809), p. 14.

Jonas, who had married a Wittenberg girl in February 1522 and who wrote in defence of marriage at Luther's request, argued that "no one knows better what men suffer in raising a family and what the holy cross of marriage is than one who daily experiences it in his own home". For the married cleric, the home is a *"praeexercitamentum charitatis"*, a "warm-up in love" which makes possible a more skilful exercise of love towards others.[34] Booms the author of the *Defence of Priestes Mariages*:

When I praie you, was religion more in honour then when priestes were maried at will without compulsion? though diverse others having the gifte of soole lief [solitary life] continued in their gifte, not despisying others. . . . When kept they their vessels *in honore et sanctificatione* . . . more safely, then when they had the libertis of mariage for the perill of incontinencie? When was hospitalitie and residentie better kept, then when the Pastor had his familie in a place certain to move him homeward? When were their houses kept in better reparations, then when they were resident? When had the people more relief by them then when they kept houses?[35]

The Reformation viewed the ministry ideally as an activity, not a state, and considered pastoral authority derived from the immediate community of believers rather than from an "indelible character".[36] This tended to put a high premium on effective contact with the daily life of the congregation. In the early years of the Reformation the home was often as much the forced as the chosen locale of Christian service, especially among the members of the so-called "Radical Reformation". Luther spoke for common Protestant experience when in 1523 he wrote to tell the Bohemians, who had been deprived of an archbishop and ordination since 1421, that the essentials of Christian faith could be fully maintained in the "homes of laymen".[37]

The second benefit of marriage for the clergy is more individual

[34] Jonas, *op. cit.*, D 2 b.
[35] *Defence of Priestes Mariages, op. cit.*, p. 30.
[36] See Luther's treatise *Concerning the Ministry* (1523), *Luther's Works* 40, p. 35 (= *WA* 12, 190.11–31).
[37] *Ibid.*, pp. 9–10 (= *WA* 12, 171.24–37).

and psychological. The cleric who is truly celibate can concentrate solely on his ministry, and Luther concedes that his is the better way "in a worldly sense" (i.e., in terms of sheer man-hours on the job).[38] Marriage, however, does for the man who cannot "contain" what celibacy does for the man who can: it removes the (sexual) cares and distractions which impede his work. "It is no slight boon," wrote Luther three years before his own marriage, "that in wedlock fornication and unchastity are checked and eliminated. This in itself is so great a good that it alone should be enough to induce men to marry forthwith. . . ."[39] He observed that marriage made for a "sound body and a good conscience" and that women with children were "healthier, cleanlier and happier".[40]

Much Protestant ink was spent against the cruelty of imposing "that which is most foreign to human nature" upon thousands of men and women. "If you are a man," wrote Jonas, "it is no more in your power to live without a woman than it is to change your sex. . . . That inborn desire and innate affection by which men and women desire one another is not in our power to control; it is the way God has created and made us."[41] Joseph Hall (†1656), dean of Worcester, reported the hard truth learned during the reign of Mary:

> John Haywood . . . told Queen Mary, Her Clergie was sawcy; if they had not Wives, they would have Lemans. Where there is not the gift of holy Continency, how could it bee otherwise? Where the water is dammed up, and yet the streame runs full, how can it choose but rise over the banks?[42]

Hall's treatise was written in 1620 for the express purpose of showing a contemporary critic of clerical marriage "how little a well-order marriage is guiltie of deadding our spirits, or slacking our hands . . .". Hall dismissed criticism as sheer "envy of matri-

[38] *The Estate of Marriage, Luther's Works* 45, p. 47 (*WA* 10², 302.10–13).
[39] *Ibid.*, p. 43 (= *WA* 10², 299.17 ff.).
[40] *Ibid.*, p. 46 (= *WA* 10², 301.11–13).
[41] Jonas, *op. cit.*, C 1 b, D 1 b.
[42] *The Honor of the Married Clergie Maintayned Against the Malicious Challenges of C.E. (= Cavillator Egregius) Masse-Priest* (London, 1620), p. 288 (copy in Yale's Beineke Library).

moniall fruitfulnesse".[43] The treatise closed with a reproduction of Erasmus' plea to the bishop of Basle that the Church be flexible with its strictly "humane constitutions".

> If marriage might bee yeelded to those which doe not contayne, both they would live more quietly, and should preach God's word to the people with authoritie, and might honestly bring up their children, neither should the one of them bee a mutuall shame to the other.[44]

While it is true that Protestant apologists often glorified "honest husbands" by contrasting them with "fornicating friars",[45] marriage was still viewed as more than simply an outlet for sexual drives. At its best it was a new awareness of human community. "Man has strange thoughts the first year of marriage," wrote Luther. "When sitting at table he thinks, 'Before I was alone; now there are two.' Or in bed, when he wakes up, he sees a pair of pigtails lying beside him which he hadn't seen there before."[46] "It does not consist only of sleeping with a woman—everybody can do that—but keeping house and bringing up children."[47] "There must be harmony with respect to patterns of life and ways of thinking. The bonds of matrimony alone won't do it."[48] As if intentionally to give the lie to a spurious ancient tradition, Protestant leaders left touching portraits of their wives as indispensable companions in their ministry. Luther boasted simply: "I wouldn't give up my Katy for France or Venice."[49] The Puritan Richard Mather (†1669) found the death of his wife "the more grievous, in that she being a Woman of singular Prudence for the Management of Affairs, had taken off from her Husband all Secular Cares, so that he wholly devoted himself to his Study, and

---

[43] *Ibid.*, A 3 b–A 4 a, 164, 48.

[44] *Ibid.*, appendix. Cf. John B. Payne, *Erasmus: His Theology of the Sacraments* (1970), pp. 109 ff. Erasmus strongly influenced such eirenic Catholic theologians as Georg Witzel, Johann Pflug and Georg Cassander, who were prepared to make marriage a free matter. Cf. Franzen, *op. cit.*, pp. 42 ff., 47 ff.

[45] Cf. Hall, *op. cit.*, p. 42.

[46] *Tabletalk* No. 3178a (1532), *Luther's Works* 54, p. 191.

[47] *Tabletalk* No. 5513 (1542/43), *ibid.*, p. 441.

[48] *Tabletalk* No. 5524 (1542/43), *ibid.*, p. 444.

[49] *Tabletalk* No. 49 (1531), *Luther's Works* 54, p. 8.

to Sacred Imployments."[50] None was more eloquent than John
Calvin, who wrote to his friend Paul Viret at the death of his
wife:

> I have been bereaved of the best companion of my life, of one
> who, had it been so ordered, would not only have been
> the willing sharer of my indigence, but even of my death.
> During her life she was the faithful helper of my ministry.
> From her I never experienced the slightest hindrance.[51]

In spite of the rosy assessment of Protestant apologists, marriage
brought difficult personal and social changes for the clergy. At
first it meant excommunication and even imprisonment, as the
first clerics to test the marital waters in Wittenberg and Strasbourg
quickly learned.[52] Usually severe financial hardship ensued, especially for those in the villages. Although sixteenth-century Europe
was generally plagued by spiralling prices and intermittent
economic recessions, the Reformation tended to make its own
financially uncomfortable bed. It rejected as superstition the more
popular revenue-gathering devices of the medieval Church. In the
wake of Protestant polemic against indulgences, pilgrimages and
the mendicant orders, many wondered whether it was religiously
proper to back their clergy with any hand-outs whatsoever. Members of the nobility shied away from Protestant austerity; new
pastors were predominantly middle-class men with middle-class
vices and pocket-books. One-third came from the ranks of school-
teachers and sextons, with clerks, typesetters, printers and cloth-
makers following in that order.[53] Although it did not destroy its
popular character, the Peasants' War struck down some grass-
roots support of the Reformation.[54] The young Church was pushed

[50] Cited by E. S. Morgan, *The Puritan Family* (Boston, 1944).
[51] *Letters of John Calvin* 2, ed. and trans. by J. Bonnet (Philadelphia,
1858), p. 216 (= *Calvini Opera* IX, Amsterdam, 1671, p. 50).
[52] Cf. Kaweran, *op. cit.*, p. 15; M. U. Chrisman, *Strasbourg and the
Reform* (New Haven, 1967), pp. 131 ff.; R. H. Bainton, Katherine Zell,
Medievalia et Humanistica N.S. 1 (1970), pp. 3–28.
[53] P. Drews, *Der evangelische Geistliche in der deutschen Vergangenheit*
(Jena, 1905), p. 16; W. Panck, *The Heritage of the Reformation* (1961),
p. 139.
[54] Cf. F. Law, "Der Bauernkrieg und das angebliche Ende der luther-
ischen Reformation als spontaner Volksbewegung", *Luther-Jahrbuch* XXVI
(1959), pp. 109–34.

towards ever greater dependence upon existing political power.[55] When on 31 October 1525 Luther wrote Elector John of Saxony of those matters requiring immediate attention if order were to prevail, at the top of the list came the petition:

> Everywhere the pastors are poverty-stricken. No one gives, no one pays. Alms and tithes have fallen away. Incomes are either non-existent, or too little. The common man esteems neither preacher nor pastor. If bold political support of the clergy is not forthcoming from your grace, in a short time there will be no parish houses, schools or students, and God's word and service will go by the board.[56]

If the granaries had always been full in the monasteries, they were not to be so in the parish houses of Protestant clergy. Many "moonlighted" to make ends meet, thankful they had mastered a secular trade. Still in 1531 Luther could write that "the preachers are poorer than before [the Reformation], and those with wife and children are truly beggars."[57] He seems even to wonder whether he had opened a Pandora's box by attacking monastic vows.

> To me it is very annoying that monks deserting the monasteries gather here in such large numbers; and what is even more perturbing is the fact that they want to marry at once, even though this type of person is not in a position to assume the responsibility incident to the married estate. I am planning daily how a limit may be set to this.[58]

It was not until the 1540s, when the alliance between Church and State was solidified, the religious houses dissolved, and the "common chests" formed, that some upgrading and standardization of the wages of the clergy occurred.[59]

Beyond the financial straits lay the difficulty of breaking a habit which for centuries had been invested with such great religious

[55] A. Schultze, *Stadtgemeinde und Reformation* (Tübingen, 1918), pp. 50–1.
[56] Cited by Drews, *op. cit.*, p. 27.
[57] Panck, *op. cit.*, pp. 140 f.; Drews, *op. cit.*, p. 25.
[58] Letter to Spalatin, *WABr* III, 109.12–15. Cited by D. B. Miller, *The Dissolution of the Religious Houses of Hesse During the Reformation*, Yale Dissertation, 1971, p. 199. Cf. Schultze, *op. cit.*, p. 44.
[59] Cf. Drews, *op. cit.*, pp. 28 ff.; Schultze, *op. cit.*, pp. 45 f.

value. Lay tolerance and even acceptance of clerical concubinage as a relationship akin to marriage grew in the late fifteenth century.[60] Still the idea of a married clergy came easily neither to the religious nor to the laity. In the early years Luther found that it was a matter in which the conscience needed continual "fortification".[61] When the monasteries of Saxony and Hesse were later dissolved, teams of preachers prepared the way with instruction. But the psychological battle was not won during Luther's lifetime. In August 1545, he preached the marriage sermon for Sigismund of Lindenau, a cathedral dean who had been secretly married for seven years before he could summon the courage to make it public. Luther dwelt on the importance of realizing that God created men and women for marriage: when one knows and believes that, then he can be "happy and confident and... live in the holy ordinance of marriage with a good conscience and a hapy mind". And he censured the persistence of an unchristian quest for angelic perfection: "If we are going to talk about the purity and chastity which the angels possess, you will not find it anywhere, either in marriage or outside of marriage in the unmarried state; that kind of purity is gone."[62]

Clerical confusion and anxiety about marriage were doubtlessly reinforced by the indecisive stance of Emperor Charles V. Although the final recess of the Diet of Augsburg (1530) enjoined married priests to abstain from their wives and even to eject them. Imperial enforcement was delayed pending a future council of the Church.[63] Had Charles not found France and the Turks more threatening than the ecclesiastical revolt in Germany, and had not such protective umbrellas as the Schmalkaldic League formed, it is conceivable that imperial power would have forced the painful decisions upon the married clergy on the Continent that the reign of Mary forced upon married clergy in England, when, according to the *Defence of Priestes Mariages*, "twelve of sixtene

[60] B. Moeller speaks of there being "schon Anfänge einer Legalisierung und damit einer gewissen Versittlichung dieser Verbindungen". Frömmigkeit im Deutschland um 1500, *ARG* 56 (1965), p. 26.
[61] Sermon preached in Wittenberg on 11 March 1522, *Luther's Works* 51, 80 (= *WA* 103, 23.14 ff.).
[62] *Luther's Works* 51, 360, 365; cf. 362 (= *WA* 49, 799 f., 803,26–28).
[63] H. C. Lea, *An Historical Sketch of Sacerdotal Celibacy in the Christian Church* (Philadelphia, 1867), p. 429; Franzen, *op. cit.*, p. 41.

thousande" were deprived of their offices, many simply choosing to labour in secular trades rather than put away their wives.[64] By the time a weary Charles was in a position to act, the fact of clerical marriage was too permanent to remove. Protestant marriages received imperial recognition in the Augsburg *Interim of 1548*.

That the laity also had difficulty adjusting to a married clergy is especially evident in the English Reformation. Although Thomas Cranmer was secretly married and Thomas Cromwell favourably disposed towards relaxing the rule of celibacy, Henry VIII forbade clerical marriage and instituted stiff penalties for failure to observe celibate vows.[65] During the reign of Edward VI, the legal right of clerical marriage was secured, yet lay dissatisfaction remained strong. When Cranmer ordered a visitation in his province, one of the points of inquiry was: "Whether any do contemn married priests, and, for that they be married, will not receive the communion or other sacraments at their hands." On 10 February 1552, a bill was passed by Parliament defending the children of married clerics as legal heirs and not, as popular sentiment had it, bastards.[66] Mary did not drum married clergy out of the ministry without considerable popular sympathy. And although Elizabeth reinstated the right of clerical marriage and even appointed married bishops, she found a married clergy as bitter a pill as had her father. It is reported that when she turned to thank the wife of Archbishop Matthew Parker after a visit to the archiepiscopal palace, she could only say to her hostess: "And you—madam I may not call you, mistress I am ashamed to call you, so I know not what to call you—but, howsoever, I thank you."[67] A reformed clergy was one thing, a married clergy quite another.

---

[64] *Defence of Priestes Mariages*, 7 a. Lea reduces this estimate to 3,000. *Op. cit.*, p. 495. Not a few married clerics were dismissed summarily with neither a hearing nor a chance freely to choose the Queen's way.

[65] See the *Six Articles* of 1539 in *Documents of the Christian Church*, ed. by H. Bettenson (New York, 1961), pp. 330–1; Lea, *op. cit.*, pp. 477–9, 483–4.

[66] *Ibid.*, pp. 489, 491. Cf. Hughes, *op. cit.*, p. 115. On the other hand, the visitations sent out in the 1560s to enforce the reform measures of Trent in Catholic territories on the Continent often found genuine lay acceptance of married priests.

[67] Cited by Lea, *op. cit.*, p. 504.

54   STEVEN OZMENT

III. The Domestication of Religious Life

If we ask about the long-term consequence of clerical marriage in the Protestant churches, it may not be inappropriate to speak of a tendency to "domesticate" religion. Spurning asceticism and other-worldliness, Protestants embraced the home and family as the superior context for the service of God and man. The joys and sorrows of wife and children could not but have tremendous impact upon theological thinking. Experiences within the home provided analogies for understanding the deepest mysteries of God. Religion was, so to speak, brought down to earth. Luther described mothers and fathers as "apostles, bishops and priests to their children", praising parenthood as the one place where spiritual and temporal authority truly intersected.[68] Luther's views were elaborated in a long series of Protestant *Ehespiegel* in the sixteenth century, each glorifying the family as the training camp for both Church and State. Justus Menius extolled marriage as the greatest of all God's vocations, comparing the *"Kinderzucht"* of Christian parents to the erection of great cities.[69] Erasmus Alberus saw marriage as a school for the elect, ordained for the future as well as for the present life.[70] Tributes traditionally reserved for the monastic life were transferred to the estate of marriage: "Jerome's unfortunate comment, 'Virginity fills heaven, marriage the earth', must be corrected. Let us rather say, 'Connubium replet coelum, marriage fills heaven'."[71] Jeremy Taylor praised marriage as "the seminary of the Church" and "the proper scene of piety".[72] It was perhaps not accidental that the most home-minded Protestants, the New England Puritans, were also the most covenant-minded Protestants, intent on worshipping a fair and reasonable God, "a God who can be counted upon, a God who can be lived with".[73]

One of the most striking modern witnesses to a Protestant

[68] *The Estate of Marriage, Luther's Works* 45, 46 (= *WA* 10² 301.23–27).
[69] *An die hochgeborne Fürstin/Fraw Sibilla Hertzogin zu Sachsen/Oeconomia Christiana/d.i./von Christlicher Haushaltung*, Wittenberg, 1529, B 2 b, A 4 b (copy in Yale's Beineke Library).
[70] *Ein Predigt vom Ehestand* (Wittenberg, 1546), C 1 b (copy in Yale's Beineke Library).
[71] *Ibid.*, C 3 b.
[72] Taylor, *op. cit.*, pp. 12–14.
[73] P. Miller, *Errand into the Wilderness* (New York, 1964²), p. 63.

tendency to "domesticate" the religious life was the controversial nineteenth-century congregational minister, Horace Bushnell (†1876). "Religion never thoroughly penetrates life," he wrote outright, "till it becomes domestic."[74] Yale educated and deeply read in German Idealism and Romanticism, Bushnell was minister of North Church in Hartford, Connecticut. In 1846 he published a book entitled *Christian Nurture*. The book was written against Charles G. Finney and the American revivalist tradition, which defined Christian life in terms of a conversion experience, a break with the normal way of life. Wrote Bushnell in rebuttal:

> The aim, effort, and expectation should be not, as is commonly assumed, that the child is to grow up in sin, to be converted after he comes to a mature age; but that he is upon the world as one that is spiritually renewed, not remembering the time when he went through a technical experience, but seeming rather to have loved what is good from his earliest years.[75]

Bushnell was convinced that the natural and supernatural worlds were organically connected.[76] Since Pentecost the Holy Spirit had "remitted" its "extraordinary" forms and taken residence "in families". "Understand that it is the family spirit, the organic life of the house, the silent power of a domestic godliness, working... unconsciously and with sovereign effect—that it is which forms your children to God."[77] Living in an age increasingly aware of Lamarck and soon to discover Darwin, Bushnell championed a natural transmission of acquired moral characteristics from parent to child. "The character of one is actually included in that of the other, as a seed is formed in the capsule."[78] He looked forward to the day when "those sporadic cases of sanctification from the womb of which the Scripture speaks, such as that of Samuel, Jeremiah and John, are... finally... the ordinary and common fact of family development."[79]

[74] *Christian Nurture* (New York, 1871), p. 63.
[75] *Ibid.*, p. 10.
[76] Elaborated in *Nature and the Supernatural* (New York, 1858).
[77] *Christian Nurture*, pp. 130, 119.
[78] *Ibid.*, p. 27.
[79] *Ibid.*, p. 206.

For Bushnell, religion was finally a household habit. The home is "the church of childhood", a "converting ordinance", where the child learns repentance, love, duty and faith.[80] Parents occupy the office of the clergy, holding the "power of binding and loosing" over their children.[81] By their "looks, manner and ways of life", parents become the "living epistles" and sacramental vessels through which Christian virtues are infused "well nigh irresistibly" into their children.[82]

It could be argued that Bushnell exaggerated classical Protestant attitudes towards marriage and the home. Still, even conceding distortion, lines of continuity remain evident. Without its complex theological safeguards, which Bushnell did not have, the Reformation's identification with secular life can lead to the cultural Protestantism of *Christian Nurture*. Karl Barth, who was as mindful of the theological safeguards of the Reformation as he was critical of cultural Protestantism, actually encouraged a new and positive Protestant *"iudicium de votis monasticis"*. In Barth's mind, Protestant celibacy could be to the cultural Protestantism of the modern world what Protestant marriage had been to the monastic life of the medieval: a reminder of the "scandalous" character of Christian faith.[83]

Given contemporary Protestant interest in the "call of the cloister", the churches of the Reformation might be thought capable of going full circle. Having been too long at home in the world, a not insignificant number of Protestant Christians seem now to feel they have become lost in it.[84] However, if there is a lesson to be drawn from the Reformation's experience in this matter, it would seem to be this: in the final analysis, the problem of being "in but not of the world" is not a matter of being inside or outside a cloister, free from or subject to vows of celibacy.

---

[80] *Ibid.*, pp. 20–22, 77.
[81] *Ibid.*, p. 315.
[82] *Ibid.*, pp. 22, 30, 64.
[83] Barth's views are discussed by Biot, *op. cit.*, pp. 144–51.
[84] See especially P. F. Anson's treatment of the monastic movement within the Anglican Church: *The Call of the Cloister* (London, 1956). An interesting Protestant appeal for "sex without sex" is made by H. W. Richardson, *Nun, Witch, Playmate: The Americanization of Sex* (New York, 1971), pp. 127 ff.

John Lynch

Critique of the Law of Celibacy in the Catholic Church from the Period of the Reform Councils

THERE were voices in the century or two before the Reformation urging the Church to moderate its traditional discipline of obligatory celibacy.[1] In preparation for the Council of Vienne (1311), the canonist William Durandus the Younger discussed the problem of clerical incontinence.[2] Almost all the councils and many of the Roman pontiffs, he observed, have legislated against concubinage. All the penalties imposed have been of no avail in improving clerical morals. He then asked whether it would not be

---

[1] For the best recent histories with ample bibliographies see: R. Gryson, *Les origines du célibat ecclésiastique du premier au septième siècle* (Gembloux, 1970); M. Boelens, *Die Klerikerehe in der Gesetzgebung der Kirche unter besonderer Berücksichtigung der Strafe: Eine rechtsgeschichtliche Untersuchung von den Anfängen der Kirche bis zum Jahre 1139* (Paderborn, 1968); M. Boelens, "Die Klerikerehe in der kirchlichen Gesetzgebung vom II Laterankonsil bis zum Konzil von Basel", *Jus Sacrum* (Festgabe) *K. Mörsdorf zum 60. Geburstag* (Munich, 1969), pp. 593–614; M. Boelens, "Die Klerikereche in der kirchlichen Gesetzgebung zwischen den Konzilien von Basel und Trent", *Archiv für katholisches Kirchenrecht*, 138 (1969), pp. 62–81. F. Liotta, *La continenza dei chierici nel pensiero canonistico classico da Graziano a Gregorio IX* (Milan, 1971); *Sacerdoce et Célibat: Etudes historiques et théologiques* (*Bibl. Eph. Theol. Lov.*) (Louvain, 1971). A continuing bibliography on all aspects of the priestly ministry, including celibacy from January 1966, is published by the Centre de Documentation et de Récherche, 2065 ouest, rue Sherbrooke, Montréal 109, Canada. A pioneer work is still very useful: Henry C. Lea, *An Historical Sketch of Sacerdotal Celibacy in the Christian Church*, 3rd edn rev. (New York, 1907).

[2] Durandus, *Tractatus de modo generalis concilii celebrandi* (Paris, apud Clousier, 1671), Pars. II, Tit. 46, pp. 157–9.

expedient for the Western Church to follow the practice of the East with regard to the vow of continence, especially since the Eastern custom dates back to apostolic times. A century later another canonist Panormitanus (1386–1445), known as *lucerna iuris* because of his eminent authority, strongly endorsed priestly marriage.[3] Cannot the Church permit clerics to contract marriage just as the Greeks do? "I believe it can," answers Panormitanus, "and this is indubitably true for those who are not bound by an implicit or explicit vow." He argued that continence is not part of the substance of the order for secular clerics, nor is it of divine law, otherwise the Greeks would be sinning. The canonist concluded that it is not only within the power of the Church but it would be for the good of souls to make continence optional. Those who chose to remain continent would merit more by doing so voluntarily; those unwilling to be continent could marry and thus avoid the evil results which experience shows to follow from obligatory continence.

Jean Gerson (1363–1429), chancellor of the University of Paris, was one of the moving spirits behind the Councils of Pisa and Constance which eventually healed the Great Western Schism. In 1423 he wrote a four-act dialogue in which *Natura* or Reason debated with *Sophia* or Theology.[4] *Natura* asks why the vow should not be eliminated from the priesthood, since celibacy is not necessarily connected with the ministry by divine law. *Sophia* points out that one becomes a minister of revealed grace through election rather than through hereditary succession as in the Old Law. Celibacy frees one from the cares of a family and from temptations to avarice in having to provide for offspring. Fully recognizing all the evils that have resulted from broken vows, *Sophia* still maintains that true reform is not going to come from the abolition of ecclesiastical celibacy. This dialogue suggests that there was considerable pressure on the Church in the fifteenth century to make celibacy optional. No less a person than Aeneas Silvius, the future Pius II, is said to have favoured such a change

[3] Panormitanus (Nicolaus de Tudeschis). *Abbatis Panormitani commentaria in tertium decretalium librum* (Venice, apud Iuntas, 1588), III, Tit. III, c. 6 (Tomus VI, p. 25).
[4] Joannis Gersonii, *Opera Omnia* (Antwerp, 1706), *Dialogus Sophiae et Naturae super caelibatu sive castitate ecclesiasticorum*, Tome II, pp. 617–34.

in ecclesiastical discipline before he became pope.[5] In an official document concerned with the agenda of the Council of Constance (1414–1418) Cardinal Zabarella stated that if concubinage could not be effectively dealt with then it would be better to permit clerics to marry.[6]

The repudiation of ecclesiastical celibacy by Luther, Zwingli, Calvin and other reformers forced the Council of Trent to consider the question at length. The Emperor Ferdinand, the Duke of Cleves and Duke Albert of Bavaria pressed the Holy See to allow priests to marry in an effort to conciliate the Protestants.[7] Though Rome was reluctant to yield on such an important matter of discipline before the Council of Trent had an opportunity to debate its merits, consideration was shown for priests who had already sought to marry. On 31 August 1548, at the instance of Emperor Charles V, the papal nuncios in Germany were empowered to recognize such marriages with the proviso that those dispensed would cease to exercise the priestly ministry as well as any other sacred function.[8] Again when Catholicism was restored in England under Mary Tudor, Cardinal Pole in 1554 received similar faculties to dispense.[9]

Finally, in February 1563, the long-postponed issue of enforced clerical celibacy was taken up at the twenty-third session of the Council of Trent in its treatment of the Sacrament of Matrimony.[10] Eight articles summarized from works of the Reformers

---

[5] Platina, *De vitis ac gestis Summorum Pontificum*, 1645 (originally written 1479): At the Council of Trent in the General Congregation concerning the decree on matrimony, Pientinus commenting on c. 7 reaffirmed this. (*Concil. Trid.* 9, 652 n. 3.)

[6] Cardinal Zabarella, *Capita agendorum in Concilio Const. de reformatione, Magnum Oecumenicum Constantiense Concilium*, ed. H. van der Hardt (Frankfurt, 1700), col. 525.

[7] Emperor Ferdinand, *Concil. Trid.* VIII, 468, 484, 485; Duke of Cleves, *Concil. Trid.* VIII, 202; Duke Albert of Bavaria, *Concil. Trid.* 8, pp. 619–26.

[8] Pope Paul III to Bishops Petrus of Fano, Aloysius of Verona and Sebastianus of Ferentino, *Nuntiatur Berichte aus Deutschland*, Ser. I, Vol. 10, pp. 461–3.

[9] Bulla papae Julii potestatem concedens cardinali Polo Anglicam ecclesiae Romanae reuniendi, *Concilia Magnae Britanniae et Hiberniae ab anno 1546–1717* (London, 1737), pp. 91–3.

[10] Hefele-Leclercq, *Histoire des conciles*, 10, p. 507. See also E. Ferasin, *Matrimonio e Celibato al Concilio di Trento* (Rome, 1970); A. Franzen,

were proposed to the Council Fathers. The fifth article stated that marriage is not to be considered lower than chastity but to be preferred to it and that God bestows on spouses a greater grace than on others. The sixth article proposed that Western priests be permitted to marry, "vow or ecclesiastical law notwithstanding; that to maintain the opposite is to condemn matrimony; that all be able to contract marriage who do not feel themselves to have the gift of chastity".[11]

The congregation of minor theologians began to discuss the two articles on 4 March 1563. The rejection of Article 5 was almost a foregone conclusion. On the basis of Scripture (chiefly 1 Cor. 7), patristic testimony, and a comparison of the ends of marriage and of virginity, speaker after speaker argued for the superiority of virginity. Article 6 received a much more extensive treatment. There was almost universal agreement that the priesthood of its nature demanded complete dedication to God in prayer, preaching and the administration of the sacraments. Whatever distracted from this orientation, as marriage certainly did, was prohibited. Celibacy really added no obligation that was not required by the priesthood itself. Though there was diversity of opinion whether the obligation of celibacy resulted from a vow or from the simple reception of the order, the practical effect was the same. The majority of theologians thought that the obligation was of ecclesiastical rather than of divine law. Even if the possibility of dispensing from the obligation of celibacy was recognized in principle, there was general reluctance to favour such action. (None of the speakers, be it noted, came from the Germanies, where the problem was particularly acute and the pressure for relaxation most insistent.) The theologians were in effect upholding the traditional discipline but leaving the door open for a married clergy in some areas. As for the Greeks, the theologians generally refrained from any direct attack, though a few speakers did refer to the Oriental practice in disparaging terms.[12]

Zölibat und Priesterehe in der Auseinandersetzung der Reformationszeit und der katholischen Reform des 16. Jahrhunderts (Münster, 1969).

[11] *Concil. Trid.* 9, n. 5, p. 380.

[12] P. Delhaye, "Brèves remarques historiques sur la législation du célibat ecclésiastique", *Studia Moralia* 3 (1965), pp. 389-94.

On 20 July the congregation of theologians proposed the following canons to the Fathers of the Council:[13]

If anyone says that Western clerics who have received sacred orders, or religious who have solemnly professed chastity, can validly contract matrimony, ecclesiastical law or vow notwithstanding, and that to maintain the opposite is only to condemn matrimony; and that all can contract marriage who do not feel themselves to have the gift of chastity, although they have vowed it: let him be anathema. (Canon 7)

If anyone says that matrimony must be placed before virginity or celibacy, and that it is not better and more blessed to remain in virginity or celibacy, than to be joined in matrimony, let him be anathema. (Canon 9)

These proposals had to be reviewed and re-presented four times before winning approval in the twenty-fourth session. Much of the discussion concerned the deletion of the word *occidentalis*. A majority of bishops voted for its deletion, but not all for the same reason. Some wanted to emphasize that celibacy was of divine institution which would not be the case if a different practice were recognized for the Eastern Church. Some bishops wanted to keep *occidentalis* since Greek priests do contract a valid marriage even if they are deprived of their priestly function. In the ninth Canon it was decided to speak of the "conjugal state and the virginal state", rather than to say merely, "If anyone says that matrimony must be placed before virginity or celibacy". The third and fourth drafts concerned the addition of a scriptural exhortation: "Since God does not deny it [the gift of chastity] to those rightly seeking it, nor does he suffer us to be tempted beyond that which we are able to bear." On 11 November 1563, the canons as amended were finally approved.[14]

Meanwhile the Emperor Ferdinand continued to urge—what he considered two essential concessions for winning over the Protestants—the chalice for the laity and a married clergy.[15] The conciliar discussions on extending the chalice to the laity resulted

---

[13] *Concil. Trid.* 9, p. 640.
[14] *Concil. Trid.* 9, p. 968 (Denz.–Schön. 1809, 1810).
[15] G. Constant, *Concession à l'Allemagne de la communion sous les deux espèces* (Paris, 1923), 2 vols.

in a stalemate, so that the question was left to the Pope for resolution. On 14 February 1564, after the close of the Council, the Emperor in conjunction with Albert of Bavaria wrote to the Pope requesting the two concessions in order to save the Church in Germany. When Rome granted the chalice but deferred action on celibacy, Ferdinand again wrote on 17 June 1564 that the chalice was useless if the bishops could not provide unmarried priests; allowance had to be made for those clergymen who had taken wives. Upon the death of the Emperor Ferdinand in that same year, his son Maximilian II continued to agitate for a married clergy. Pope Pius IV feared that such a dispensation would prove to be a disaster, yet he did not want to push the Emperor into the camp of the Protestants. The Pope's hand was strengthened when Philip II ordered the Spanish Cardinal Pacheco vigorously to oppose any relaxation of the law of celibacy. The Pope resorted to a series of delaying tactics during the course of which he died. From instructions given to the papal nuncios it seems incontestable, however, that the Pope was ready to use his dispensatory power if he could be persuaded that such action was necessary for the conversion of Germany. Under the next Pope, Pius V, all negotiations ceased.[16]

On the doctrinal and juridical level the Council of Trent successfully withstood the concerted assault of the reformers on clerical celibacy. On the practical level, too, it succeeded, as no previous Council had, in bringing about general observance of the discipline. Perhaps more than to any other single cause the effectiveness of Trent may be attributed to the seminary system which it inaugurated. Only with a rigorous training beginning at youth and carried on over a long period of time under constant supervision and careful selection could there be any hope of ordaining candidates prepared to assume such a complete dedication.[17]

The victory of Trent was not immediately apparent.[18] Though the Council had spoken, the problem of clerical celibacy was far

[16] L. Pastor, *The History of the Popes*, ed. R. F. Kerr, 16 (St. Louis, 1928), pp. 112-37.
[17] J. A. O'Donohoe, *Tridentine Seminary Legislation: Its Sources and Its Formation* (Louvain, 1957).
[18] See G. Alberigo, "The Council of Trent: New Views on the Occasion of Its Fourth Centenary", *Concilium*, Sept. 1965.

from settled in many Catholic areas. The Tridentine decrees long remained unpromulgated and ineffective in many countries, largely because of political interference. In many places, too, the lower clergy persisted in their accustomed vices. The Synod of Osnabruck in 1625 blamed the stubbornness of the heretics on the immorality of the clergy who openly supported their children from the patrimony of the Church.[19] A few years later (1631) at a synod in the same diocese, an orator inveighed against priests who not only enjoyed female companionship but dignified their women with the name of wives.[20] A synod held at Cambray in 1631 was disposed to waive clerical immunity by suggesting that the secular arm be called upon to remove concubines of the clergy.[21] As late as 1652 the bishop of Münster could complain that his clergy persisted in concubinage to the scandal of the faithful and the destruction of the authority of religion.[22]

Not only were the decrees of Trent passively resisted, but the frontal attack on the discipline of celibacy continued unabated. The Sorbonne had to censure several propositions taken from works on moral theology and history. In 1665 it condemned the opinion that a professed religious who believes he has received a dispensation from God to marry may licitly do so. The next year it denounced the thesis that up to and including the time of Pope Leo IX (1049–1054) priests and bishops married just as the laity did. Throughout the seventeenth century hundreds of books dealing with the subject of celibacy poured from the presses of Europe,[23] clear evidence that Trent had not buried the issue. Some of the treatises were continuations of the controversy between Protestants and Catholics carried over from the previous century. Others, pro and con, were in response to new philosophical and scientific currents stirred up by Descartes and Newton.

---

[19] Schannat-Hartzheim, *Concilia Germaniae*, 9, pp. 351–2.
[20] *Concilia Germaniae*, 9, p. 431.
[21] *Concilia Germaniae*, 9, p. 562.
[22] *Concilia Germaniae*, 9, p. 787.
[23] A. de Roskovany, *Coelibatus et breviarium: duo gravissima clericorum officia, e monumentis omnium seculorum demonstrata. Accessit completa literatura*, 11 vol. (Pest-Neutra, 1861–1881), and *Supplementa ad collectiones monumentorum et literature* III. *De coelibatu et breviario* (Neutra, 1888). For the condemnations of the Sorbonne see Vol. 6, No. 2347 and No. 2380, 2381. For a survey of the literature of the seventeenth century see Vol. 4, pp. 117–18.

64   JOHN LYNCH

An instance of an old controversy viewed from a new perspective after the Wars of Religion may be seen in the correspondence of two eminent figures of the age. The bishop of Meaux,
Bossuet, and the philosopher Leibniz negotiated for over twenty
years (1679–1702) in hopes of working out a reunion between
the Catholic and Lutheran Churches.[24] The two were not working
in isolation but as part of a definite movement towards reunion
which had the encouragement of Pope Innocent XI. As a basis
for discussion Leibniz sent to Bossuet a memorandum prepared
by a Lutheran theologian. One point calls attention to the alarm
Protestant ministers and people have over the law of celibacy.
Bossuet in reply noted that the Maronites of Syria had been received into full communion without being forced to change their
rites. No difficulty has ever been raised about Greek priests enjoying the use of marriage. The Greeks themselves do not recognize
marriage after ordination and their bishops are obliged to celibacy. There were, of course, more fundamental issues on which
Bossuet and Leibniz could not agree, but the law of celibacy at
least was not standing in the way of reunion.

It was inevitable that the spirit of the Enlightenment would
exert a profound influence on the thought of Catholic intellec-
tuals.[25] This revolutionary movement which originated in the
Netherlands and England was to shift the culture of Europe
from an ecclesiastical and theological orientation to a wholly
secular one. With unreserved confidence in reason and science, an
optimistic view of man and his universe, the Enlightenment took
a radically critical stance towards all patterns of thought and
values. Man's fulfilment was of primary concern. In its distinc-
tively Catholic form, the Enlightenment stimulated a renewal in
the Church: reform in the liturgy, an upgrading of clerical
education, and an attack on superstitition and credulity.

During the eighteenth century, reflecting the critical mood of
the times, there appeared over one thousand treatises challenging
or defending ecclesiastical celibacy.[26] Almost anyone with preten-

[24] See F. Gaquère, Le dialogue irénique Bossuet–Leibniz: La réunion
des Eglises en échec (1691–1702) (Paris, 1966).
[25] See G. Schwaiger, "Catholicism and the Enlightenment", Concilium,
Sept. 1967.
[26] Roskovany, De coelibatu et breviario, 4, No. 1065-1795; Vol. 7, No.
5023b-5312.

sions of being a philosopher considered it a prerequisite to hold celibacy up to ridicule. In France and Italy, as well as in Germany, propagandists for the abolition of celibacy were numerous. They claimed that since the early Church knew no such prohibition, nothing prevented clerics from marrying even without a dispensation. For the most part they argued from the natural-law provision that every man had a God-given right to marry. Additional reasons were found in the physical make-up of man, the needs of society, therapeutic considerations, and a host of others. Some of the arguments appealing to the Greek experience did not clearly differentiate between ordaining married men and allowing priests to marry.

The popularity of such rationalists as Voltaire, Helvetius and Holbach added to persistent Gallican and Jansenist sentiments emboldened some French ecclesiastics to speak out against the ancient discipline. In 1758 Desforges, a canon Estampes, sought to prove in a two-volume work that it was more conformable to the divine ordinance (Gen. 1. 28) for priests and bishops to marry.[27] Public opinion was not yet prepared for such a radical thesis, with the result that the French Parliament had the book burned and the author confined in the Bastille. The work, however, continued to be reprinted and was soon translated into German and Italian. In defence of celibacy the Jesuit Zaccaria published at Rome in 1774 *Storia polemica del Celibato sagro da contraporsi ad alcune detestabili opere uscite a questi tempi.*[28] A few years later Gaudin, a priest of the Oratory who later married, published at Geneva (1781) *Les Inconveniens du Celibat des Prêtres, prouvés par des recherches historiques,* in which he marshals historical and philosophical evidence to show the detrimental effects of celibacy.[29] Zaccaria again replied with *Nuova giustificazione del celibato sacro dagli inconvenienti oppostogli anche ultimamente in alcuni infamissimi libri.*[30]

The French Revolution, which in many ways marks the climax of the Enlightenment, moved the question from the theoretical into the practical arena. The Constitution of 1791 provided that no profession could debar a person from marriage and that no

[27] Roskovany, 4, No. 1201.
[28] Roskovany, 4, No. 1269.
[29] Roskovany, 4, No. 1308.
[30] Roskovany, 4, No. 1470.

public official or notary could refuse to ratify a marriage on such a ground.[31] For a priest, marriage was then considered a pledge of loyalty, and continued celibacy a silent protest against the new regime. Many clerics, of course, readily took advantage of the liberal climate, others remained adamant, and a third group merely went through the formality of a civil marriage ceremony. Opposition to the abrogation of celibacy remained strong, even among the *assermentés* who had pledged themselves to the Revolution by oath. The people, too, generally rejected clerical marriage so that after the Reign of Terror one of the first efforts at reorganizing the Church was directed to the restoration of celibacy. As early as 1795, some *assermentés* bishops issued an encyclical in which clerical marriage was denounced in the strongest terms.[32] The Concordat with Napoleon in 1801 ignored the problem of clerical marriage; the internal discipline of the Church was left to itself.

After the signing of the Concordat 3,224 priests and religious petitioned either for reinstatement or for the regularization of their marriages. Of these well over two thousand chose marriage.[33] At the time Talleyrand, the minister of foreign affairs and former bishop of Autun, sought a dispensation for himself. Cardinal Consalvi transmitted the decision of Rome on 30 June 1802:[34]

> I should have wished, truly, that Your Excellency's desires could have been entirely fulfilled and that the Brief could have included the permission to marry; but how was this to be when, in eighteen centuries of Church history, there is not a single instance of such a concession? . . . No consecrated bishop has ever been dispensed in order to marry. . . . Not only is there no precedent in eighteen centuries but . . . there are several instances in which this permission was consistently refused by the Holy See.

[31] Duguit, L. et Monnier, *Les constitutions de la France depuis 1789* (Paris, 1898).

[32] H. Grégoire, *Histoire du mariage des prêtres en France, Particulièrement depuis 1789* (Paris, 1826), p. 109.

[33] S. Delacroix, *La réorganisation de l'Eglise de France après la Revolution 1801–1809* (Paris, I, 1962), Ch. 20; "La réconciliation des prêtres et religieux mariés", pp. 443–56.

[34] F. Mathieu, *Le concordat de 1801* (Paris, 1904), p. 348.

The arrangement at the end of the French Revolution reducing clerics to the lay state and validating their marriages marked the third and last time in modern history that the Church has authorized a general dispensation.[25]

The Hapsburg Emperor Joseph II (1780–1790) was a typical enlightened ruler who had read contemporary reform writers and determined to put their ideas into practice. He looked upon the Church as a governmental agency which had to be reorganized in the interests of efficiency, economy and simplicity. Imperial decrees replaced the old diocesan seminaries, which he considered seedbeds of superstition, with five general theological schools. Here clerical candidates were to be given instruction in secular knowledge and natural science. For all practical purposes the students were being prepared to become state officials.[26] A Study Commission recommended that celibacy be done away with in order to attract vigorous young men. Other advisers urged its abolition as a logical corollary to the Emperor's other reforms, especially the Edict of Toleration. It seems the Emperor was prepared to decree the abrogation of celibacy for priests when he abruptly forbade any further discussion of the subject in 1783.[37]

In 1802 Heinrich Ignaz Von Wessenberg, Vicar General of Constance, an ecclesiastic imbued with Enlightenment ideas, began to mould his diocese in accord with the new spirit. He reformed the breviary and missal, introduced the Mass in German, removed statues from churches, restricted pilgrimages and religious orders. He revamped the seminary at Meersburg, replacing scholasticism with contemporary philosophy. Then, with official approbation, the principle of ecclesiastical celibacy was openly attacked.[28] At the seminary of Rottenburg, also, there was vigorous agitation for the abolition of celibacy, enthusiastically supported by the students. In 1828 the lay professors of Freiburg,

---

[35] J. A. Abo, "The Problem of Lapsed Priests", *The Jurist* 23 (1963), pp. 153–79.

[36] S. K. Padover, *The Revolutionary Emperor: Joseph II of Austria*, 2nd rev. edn. (New York, 1967), pp. 164–5.

[37] E. Wangermann, *From Joseph II to the Jacobin Trials*, 2nd edn. (Oxford, 1969), p. 15.

[38] H. Savon, *Johann Adam Möhler, The Father of Modern Theology*, trans. C. McGrath (New York, 1966), p. 10.

convinced that something had to be done to raise the moral and spiritual level of the clergy, petitioned the government to permit priests to marry. A large number of the clergy as well as the seminarians added their signatures to the petition. An association was formed in the Diocese of Rottenburg to work for the repeal of the ecclesiastical law of celibacy.[39]

Just at that time Johann Adam Möhler, sometimes called the Father of Modern Theology, began his literary career in the *Theologische Quartalschrift*. One of his first articles (1826) was entitled "Some Thoughts on the Diminishing Number of Priests and Certain Related Questions". In a highly critical tone he rejoices that secularization has reduced the number of priests; one of the Church's greatest evils has always been an excessive clerical population. "From the very nature of things, there can only be a few priests. . . . Think of celibacy. How few there are who are able and eager to understand it. Even if in this respect there are to outward appearances many priests, interiorly they are very few." Two years later, in *Der Katholik*, Möhler sarcastically assailed the Baden clergy who thought that the cure for lack of zeal and spirituality was in the taking of wives. Celibacy, Möhler insists, arose in the beginning spontaneously as an inner necessity for those destined to the constant service of God. It was only after moral lapses occasioned by the barbarian invasions that the Church felt constrained to spell out this obligation in law. The practice of the Greek Church, which permits the ordination of married men, does not argue to the contrary. The case of a man who marries with no thought of the priesthood and then is called to the service of the people (as the Greeks permit) is quite different from the case of one called to the priesthood before he is married. As for the contention that the Church has no right to deprive its priests of a fundamental liberty, Möhler replies that the Church has the right to reserve the priesthood for those who have already received the highest religious consecration, the gift of virginity. He then confronts the objection that celibacy stunts growth in love, isolating a person in his own selfishness. Wife and children, too, Möhler insists, can be but a projection of a man's selfishness. Since selfishness is bound up with our nature,

[39] See *Theol. Quartl.* 150 (1970), pp. 40–1.

purely natural growth or development cannot free us from it. Only through grace can self-love be transcended to Christian love, a transformation which can occur through priestly celibacy just as through Christian marriage.[40]

Agitation reached such a strident pitch that Pope Gregory XVI was compelled to take note of it in his Encyclical *Mirari vos* of 15 August 1832. He called for support in the face of a "most detestable conspiracy against clerical celibacy" (*foedissima conjuratio*) which was becoming more widespread day by day. In collusion with some of the most depraved *philosophes* are to be found ecclesiastics swept away by the allurements of pleasure, oblivious of their calling. Publicly and in some places repeatedly they have addressed appeals to rulers for the abolition of this most sacred discipline. Ashamed to treat at length of these "base attempts", the Pope beseeched the bishops to do all in their power to resist the wiles of the wanton and to preserve intact this most important law.[41] The next pontiff, Pius IX, also felt obliged in his first encyclical, *Qui pluribus* of 9 November 1846, to censure the "vicious conspiracy" against the sacred celibacy of clerics which is promoted by churchmen overcome by the blandishments of pleasure.[42] A few years later he denounced those who asserted that marriage was a higher calling than virginity.[43] The famous "Syllabus of Errors" of 1864 called attention again to these earlier condemnations.[44]

By no means was the movement to eliminate celibacy limited to Germany. An English visitor to Florence in 1865 wrote a series of letters about the religious reform movement in Italy which appeared in *The Guardian*, and which were published the next year in book form.[45] He reports that at Naples an organization called the *Società Emancipatrice e di Mutuo Soccorso del Sacerdozia Italiano* was formed with the *Emancipatore Cattolico* as its organ.[46] In a *Memorandum* the objectives of the reform were

---

[40] H. Savon, *Johann Adam Möhler*, pp. 70–9.
[41] *Acta Gregorii Papae* (Rome, 1901), I, pp. 169–74.
[42] *Acta Pii IX Pontificis Maximi* (Rome, 1854), Pars Prima I, 13.
[43] *Ibid.*, I, 281.
[44] No. 74 n. *Acta Pii IX* III, 715 (Denz.–Schön. 2974).
[45] W. Talmadge, *Letters from Florence on the Religious Reform Movements* (London, 1866).
[46] *Ibid.*, p. 160.

stated. Prominent among them was the abolition of clerical celibacy. The *Memorandum* claimed twenty-four branch societies in various parts of the kingdom with almost a thousand priests and as many laymen as members. Dr Prota, an ex-Dominican, points out in the *Emancipatore* that under a recently enacted civil law no priest can be prevented by his bishop from contracting marriage. Prota urges priests to marry and continue in the exercise of their ministry, "and the more who do so at once and simultaneously, the safer for all, for the bishops will venture the less to prosecute you in face of public opinion".[47] The organization working for the reform of clerical discipline was closely tied in with the national unification movement which would disrupt the First Vatican Council and end the temporal power of the papacy.

Though Vatican Council I, the first Ecumenical Council since Trent, enacted no decree on the subject, several interesting comments on celibacy were made in connection with the Council. On 18 August 1869, four Lutheran pastors in the name of many evangelicals from Saxony presented the bishop of Paderborn with a petition that the Pope remove two impediments which seemed to them to stand in the way of reunion, namely, the law of celibacy and the denial of the cup to the laity.[48] The petition urged that the Eastern discipline be adopted throughout the whole Church so that married men could be ordained priests. Conceding the advisability of preserving a distinct priestly caste, the petitioners proposed that priests be allowed to marry only the daughters of priests and schoolmasters and that the priests use a chalice distinct from that used by the laity. The Lutheran petitioners seemed to have in mind a Christian counterpart to the Levitical priesthood.

A short schema of three chapters *De vita et honestate clericorum* was presented to the Council by the preparatory commission. The schema was debated in eight General Congregations of the Council from 25 January to 8 February 1870 (Mansi, 50, 517–700). In the only reference to celibacy the document reaffirmed the penalties enacted by Trent for violators and ordered the bishops to preserve in their achives a record of the evidence, especially when they proceeded in an extra-judicial manner. Some

[47] *Ibid.*, pp. 166–7.
[48] *Collectio Lacensis* (Fribourg, 1890), 7, pp. 1137–44.

bishops wanted to delete any reference to concubinage lest people think this was a common vice among the clergy. Others just as firmly insisted that the situation not be glossed over, especially if it were rampant in many places. The archbishop of Gran, Hungary, implored the Council not to miss the opportunity of declaring the powerful witness value of celibacy, "for we know how many books have appeared lately attacking celibacy with the express statement that this Council should abolish it; we must respond, Never!"[49]

The Armenian archbishop of Mardin (Mesopotamia) urged the Council to impose celibacy on all the Orientals. He then enumerated the evils that resulted from a married clergy: they provide more for their families than for their churches; they seek to adorn their wives more than the sacred altars; they care more for their children than for the faithful entrusted to them. The archbishop added that he was aware of these evils from personal experience but hastened to add, *juxta meam aetatem loquor.*[50]

With so many opinions to be reconciled, the Council proceeded to discuss the next schema which dealt with a proposed universal catechism on the model of Bellarmine's in order to replace the numerous diocesan catechisms then in use.[51] Neither the proposal on priestly life nor the one on the catechism was ever brought to a vote. The Council disbanded at the approach of Victor Emmanuel's troops.

After the Council a number of Catholic priests and laity, chiefly in German-speaking areas, refused to accept the decrees on papal infallibility and primacy. In September 1871 at Munich three hundred representatives met to organize the Old Catholic movement. The next year a similar congress was held at Cologne. Eventually a number of autonomous episcopates were established which have as a common doctrinal basis the Declaration of Utrecht. Since 1889 the Old Catholic archbishop of Utrecht has been president of the International Old Catholic Congress.[52]

---

[49] *Mansi* 50, p. 533.
[50] *Mansi* 50, pp. 683–4.
[51] *Mansi* 50, p. 1144.
[52] C. B. Moss, *The Old Catholic Movement: Its Origins and History* (London, 1948), pp. 234 ff.

Compulsory celibacy for the clergy was abolished by the Old Catholics in Switzerland as early as 1875. In Germany a significant modification was introduced in 1877. Permission to marry must come from the bishop (with provision for an appeal to the synod, in case of his refusal); this permission is not to be given within six years of ordination to the priesthood or within three years of admission to the diocese in case of a priest ordained elsewhere. In 1880 the first Austrian Old Catholic Synod eliminated compulsory celibacy, but the obligation was not removed in Holland until 1922.[53]

Ignaz von Döllinger's affiliation with the Old Catholic Movement remained ambiguous; he was reluctant to promote organized schism. The innovations introduced by the Old Catholics led him to dissociate himself from the movement; the abandonment of celibacy played a crucial role. He wrote to a close Anglican friend: "You in England cannot understand how completely engrained it is into our people that a priest is a man who sacrifices himself for the sake of his parishioners. He has no children of his own in order that all the children in the parish may be his children. His people know that his small wants are supplied, and that he can devote all his time and thought to them."[54]

Döllinger was far from being the only historical theologian to find himself at odds with the Church in the closing decades of the nineteenth century. In 1882 the brothers Theiner published an attack on enforced celibacy stressing the evils it had caused, *Einfuhrung der erzwungenen Ehelosigkeit bei den christlichen Geistlichen und ihre Folgen.* Augustin Theiner agreed to repudiate the work after its condemnation by Rome.[55] A few years later the historico-critical approach to theology would culminate in Modernism.[56] Pope Pius X later noted in *Pascendi* (1907) that one

---

[53] *Ibid.*, pp. 255, 257, 274-6, 295.
[54] A. Plummer, *The Expositor*, 2 (1890), p. 470. See H. Thurston, "Celibacy of the Clergy", *Catholic Encyclopedia*, III (New York, 1908), pp. 481-482 for more extensive citations.
[55] H. Hoffmann, *Lex. Theol. Kir.* 10 (1965), p. 15.
[56] Ernest Renan, the rationalist, offers unexpected witness to the exemplary morality of priests in France. On the eve of his ordination to the priesthood he finally admitted to himself that he no longer believed and left the Church. Looking back almost forty years later (1883), he vouched

of the goals of the Modernists was to eliminate sacerdotal celibacy.[57] Treatises of two French priests were soon placed on the index of forbidden books: *Le clergé contemporain et le célibat* by Dolonne and *Le mariage des prêtres* by Jules Claraz.[58] About the same time a reputed historian of religion, Paul-Louis Couchoud, circulated a brochure entitled *Les prêtres et le mariage, un Décret de Léon XIII autorisant le mariage des prêtres de l'Amerique latine.*[59] There is not the slightest evidence that any such papal document was ever issued.

Baron von Hügel, however, a great lay theologian and loyal Catholic, friend of the leading Modernists Loissy and Tyrrell, held both marriage and celibacy in high esteem. He recognized clearly the dangers of extremism: the attitude that downgrades marriage "at once weakens the beauty not only of marriage but of celibacy as well". Von Hügel was willing to grant that "the question of life-long, obligatory celibacy is a grave one" and that "certain modifications of the discipline now required by the Roman Catholic Church in its Latin rite may be seriously desirable",[60] but he refused to allow priests who had married to be associated with any reform movement in which he had any part. In a letter referring to the case of the ex-Carmelite Père Hyacinthe Loyson, he warned George Tyrrell against letting a married priest join the Modernist movement: "For whatever one may think, *in abstracto*, of celibacy, a priest who abandons it puts himself out of court for pleading for the difficult reform we require." In another letter three years later Von Hügel wrote:[61] "The reform of the celibacy question demands very delicate handling ... those who have gone and settled it, for their own

---

for the probity of its ministers: "The fact is that what is commonly said about clerical morality is in my experience completely devoid of any foundation. I spent thirteen years under the tutelage of priests without seeing the shadow of a scandal." *Souvenirs d'enfance et de jeunesse* (Paris, 1893), p. 139.

[57] *Acta Sancta Sedis* 40 (1907), pp. 631–2.

[58] Decree vs Dolonne 22 Jan. 1912 (*AAS* IV, 56); decree vs Claraz 6 May 1912 (*AAS* IV, 369).

[59] *L'ami du clergé* 53 (1936), p. 312.

[60] "On Certain Central Needs", *Essays and Addresses*, 2 (1926), p. 94.

[61] *Selected Letters 1896–1924*, ed. with memoir by B. Holland (New York, 1928), pp. 142, 183–5.

case, out-of-hand, have disqualified themselves for any really useful leadership in the particular work we have at hand."

In the period immediately after World War I a number of priests in the Jednota movement of Czechoslovakia claimed the right to marry. A delegation went to Rome to obtain the abolition of celibacy. Pope Benedict XV replied in the strongest possible language (1920) that the Church considered celibacy to be of such importance that they should not entertain any hope that the Church would ever abolish it.[62] The priests then proclaimed their independence of the Holy See and established a national Church.[63]

In recent years, usually in the case of convert ministers, the papacy has in conformity with the Greek tradition permitted the ordination of married men. The Second Vatican Council has given legal sanction to this practice by providing in the restoration of the diaconate that this order is able "to be conferred upon men of mature age, even upon those living in the married state".[64] The present controversy about obligatory celibacy for the priesthood dates from Pope John's announcement of Vatican II in 1959. The Italian Dominican R. Spiazzi in commenting upon this announcement published some objections to the present discipline.[65] Though he quickly pledged his own support for the maintenance of the traditional law, the dyke had been breached and a torrent of articles, books, surveys and discussions has followed.

From this brief survey it is evident that the debate about celibacy did not end at the twenty-fourth Session of the Council of Trent. Serious theologians from time to time during the past four centuries have questioned the grounds as well as the appropriateness for the imposition of this discipline. Some of the reasons advanced in the past, such as apostolic origin or cultic purity, have as a consequence been largely abandoned. Though authorities in the Church have resisted the re-opening of the question, resorting to the Index and other ecclesiastical censures,

[62] Benedict XV, *Allocutio*, 16 Dec. 1920 (*AAS* 12, pp. 585-8).
[63] *AAS* 12 (1920), p. 33; *AAS* 12 (1920, p. 37).
[64] *Lumen Gentium* No. 29.
[65] R. Spiazzi commenting on announcement of Vatican II, *Monitor Ecclesiasticus* 84 (1959), pp. 389-92; French trans., *La documentation catholique* 57 (1960), cols. 402-4.

the controversy has not been laid definitively to rest. Almost every reform movement, every attempt at *aggiornamento*, has been forced to take up the issue. More recently a modification of obligatory celibacy has been urged, not so much because of abuses or as a concession to human frailty, but out of ecumenical concern. Reunion without such accommodation appears highly unlikely. As in the past, the debate on celibacy does not go on in isolation but in the larger context of the place of the ministry in the Christian community.

Robert L. Stern

How Priests came to be Celibate:
An Oversimplification

ONCE upon a time there was a man of God called Jesus. He announced to the oppressed of his land the good news of the establishment of a revolutionary new order for men and human society. He spoke of this in terms of the establishment of the reign of God in the lives of individuals and among men. He proclaimed this news in his personal style of life and behaviour as well as in his conversation, and he practised what he preached. He was so consistent that he died rather than compromise his commitment of obedience and openness to the will of God and loving service and responsiveness to his fellow men.

Jesus not only provided us with insight, vision and truth; he not only taught us and displayed a way of life leading to full liberation, maturity and self-realization as a son of God, but shared with us his own spirit and vitalized our human efforts so as to bring us to a new quality and intensity of life.

During his life, Jesus' magnetic personality, attractive style of life and clear, strong teaching won him many friends and admirers (and enemies, too). Gradually he won many disciples; he gave them much attention and concern and asked them to commit themselves to allowing God to reign in their lives and to share with others what they had received from him. In effect, he was promoting a total restructuring and renewal of the whole of human society; the implications of his teaching were gradually appreciated in later years.

In the land where Jesus lived, some of his co-religionists were prompted to live quiet and peaceful lives in community at the edge of the desert. Even though they sprang from a tradition of esteem for virility and family, some of them were inclined to seek their fulfilment and creative self-expression in a special commitment to God and community service. Perhaps their motives were partly rooted in quirks of personality, in the pressures of their troubled times, as well as in the insistent demands of the Lord himself. Who can say, whether in this or in similar situations?

In the culture of the ancient Eastern lands many traditions had been developing, particular to and distinctly of those times and places. For example, in some societies the castration of men was accepted for certain reasons, and eunuchs had special and distinctive roles. One practical task was that of harem attendant; for a man jealous of his many wives a reliable eunuch was a useful collaborator. Eunuchs often held the most prominent administrative and military positions in governments; for a king jealous of his authority and fearful for his throne, a man necessarily without dynastic ambitions was a great help. In the East the curious concept developed of some men becoming eunuchs for the sake of the service of the kingdom.

Jesus himself, of course, was no court official or eunuch; as a matter of fact he never married, although he certainly was a man who loved and was deeply loved. He spoke of an ideal of men committing themselves, as though they were eunuchs, to the service of the kingdom of God, and his life displayed this kind of generosity and strength of purpose.

The disciples of Jesus certainly esteemed a life rooted so deeply in God that it found no time or inclination to marry and raise a family. Not only had they been challenged to this ideal by the teaching and example of Jesus, but their own Jewish and Eastern traditions supported the ideal in some measure. Another influence in their attitude towards marriage and the family was a peculiar and aberrant view of sexuality. Although the Hebrew traditions were reasonable and integral in their concept of man, the Greco-Roman world and culture in which the followers of Jesus multiplied was deeply affected by a philosophy of man overly emphasizing the spiritual, at the price of a gradual disparagement of the corporeal, quality of his nature. Some idealistic men tended to contemn sexuality just as, curiously, others from similar reasons tended to distort and overindulge it.

At any rate, over the years certain distinctive life-styles began to develop among the followers of Jesus, involving a commitment to the single, celibate life. Whether out of an attitude of escapism, a psychological inability to bear with the urban society of the day, a literal acceptance of the Gospel's counsels, or a deep hunger for uninterrupted attention to God, his designs and his creation, some men went to the deserts and lonely places to be solitaries.

As their fame grew, they attracted attention, admirers and followers, and for a while this pattern of solitary life grew and deeply touched the feelings of those who saw in such a style a strength and commitment to God that they were incapable of. Curiously enough, then, these hermits who put themselves on the margin of human society ended with a real social function after all!

Over the years this eremitical style gradually expanded into another: small fraternities or communities of celibates sharing some aspects of their life and work together. This development apparently became consolidated into what came to be known as the "monastic life". But, in this style several new notions and tendencies were at play. The monastery was first a stable community, and it saw itself at the service of the Lord by the quality of its life and prayer, and at the service of men by witnessing to the possibilities of human association in the Spirit, and by providing an oasis of spiritual refreshment in an increasingly arid world.

Perhaps it was this latter awareness that led to monasteries growing closer to civilized centres; the desert is not so much the wasteland as the wasted human society without the light and life of Christ. At any rate, the monastery soon became a centre of civilization, and the community of celibates saw themselves more and more with a responsibility and service to others outside.

Jesus' original followers saw themselves not only as his disciples and spiritual heirs but as collaborators in his mission. This view sprang not only from the contagious enthusiasm for the kind of life they lived but from the Lord's own mandate. He had commissioned them all, and particularly his twelve special disciples, to witness to his teaching by word and example and so to spread the kingdom of God among men.

One of the distinctive qualities of the life of Jesus was service. He constantly displayed a disposition to place himself at the service of others, and he held forth to his followers the ideal of total service as the greatest stature of a man. His teaching was that loving service of God and men knows no limits of quality or of quantity; he offered the example of even menial attention to others and of total self-divestment, even to the gift of his own life. In a day when the Messiah was being sought as the King, Jesus revealed him as the Suffering Servant and called on his followers to serve in the same way.

This sense of mandated service and of mission sparked and drove his followers. Not only did they place themselves at the direct service of the Word by their teaching and preaching, but the quality of their lives gave testimony to God's reign as well. They counselled and consoled one another, prayed and suffered together, shared their possessions and waited upon one another. Loving service became the identifying mark of the early Christian community.

Although all Christians shared the one responsibility for the spreading of the kingdom, each could not do all things. Jesus himself had picked certain men to have a special share of responsibility for the common mission and a particular role of service. Gradually a variety of specialized services or ministries developed in the early Christian community. Some were outward-directed in the sense they involved an approach to Jews and Gentiles who did not know Christ; others were inward-directed and were services of administration, co-ordination and organization of the Christian community itself, ranging from presiding at the Eucharist to managing its monies.

From an unconscious blending of several roles and functions—the Old Testament offerer of sacrifice, the proclaimer of God's will to men, the disciple of Jesus, the apostolic servant, the presbyter-bishop, the presider over the Eucharist—gradually emerged the figure we know as a priest. At first he was a married man or single, and he worked at this priestcraft only sometimes or constantly. But, within a short time, as stable Christian communities flourished, the need for permanent and fully committed persons with public responsibility became felt. Soon the priests and other ministers, married or single, became a kind of class within the Church.

With the establishment of the Christian way as the state religion in the fourth century, Christian communities became legitimate, multiplied and were a visible presence in the larger society. Their committed workers and leaders took on a certain civil status and authority. In a world whose tradition identified authority civil and sacred, priests and other ministers became public functionaries of a new, Christian society. As the affluence and influence of the Church developed, the inward-directed dimensions of ministry loomed ever more important. Also, as society at large became more Christian, the parameters of civil and ecclesiastical society blended as one, and the outward-directed, apostolic functions of ministry became more rare. The result of all these changes was the gradual bureaucratization of the ministerial class into a kind of ecclesiastical civil service, a corps of Churchmen known as the "clergy".

A necessary concomitant of this evolution was that the role of the priest gradually merged with that of the priest-cleric; the demands of being churchman pressed upon the root vocation to be a man of God. The Church, of course, is the assemblage of servants of the Lord, but inevitably the Church needs to be served as well. Whether out of a confusion of the Kingdom with the Church, the instrument for its promotion, or whether out of the decay of classical society and the stratification of roles in the Dark Ages, the concept of the clerical priest became a familiar and comfortable one, and he gradually assumed more and more of the responsibilities that once were the prerogative of every Christian.

In spite of this institutionalization of the priest's role, the functions of the ministry were never conceived of as separate from the person of the minister. Demands were made upon the priest to live a certain quality of life and display a certain degree of holiness appropriate to the dignity and sacredness of his calling and functions. If he held most of the Christian responsibilities in a pre-eminent way, then he pre-eminently should be a disciple of Christ. Especially, he should be celibate.

The ideal of celibacy for the priest had a variety of roots. Jesus, the one Priest of the new dispensation, never married. Also, the Lord himself counselled celibacy for the sake of the kingdom, and the example of so many religious communities testified to the permanence of this ideal. Beside lesser considerations of a socio-political or economic nature, a major influence on the development of the ideal was the Old Testament concept of a ritual, priestly purity whose spirit was not entirely unrelated to the strange and distorted notions of sexuality and sexual morality that had developed in the West. Celibacy was seen above all else as continence, and continence as an abstention from a necessarily polluting and profoundly worldly desire and behaviour. The Hebrew priest, the pagan priest, and pre-eminently the Christian priest, needed to be a man of God, a man apart, a purified man; accordingly he had to renounce or abstain from sexual behaviour.

Another current of influence was the development of the religious order priests. Monasteries had their priests—were they not Christian communities, too? As time went on, because of the esteem for the dignity of the offerer of the Eucharist and the administrator of the sacraments, more and more monks became priests. Another style of priest was developing, closer to its roots as disciple and apostle, and deeply tied to another ideal of celibacy as it had developed in turn from a variety of perceptions and situations—the priest-monk.

The monastic priest paradoxically enough was a layman; that is to say, he first rooted his vocation in the general discipleship of Christ and was not a publicly commissioned leader and civil servant of the ecclesiastical community. But as the monasteries corporately became the prime institutions of the Church, as the roles of service of the monks to the outside community flourished, and as the quality of clerical priests declined, the monastic priests gradually slipped into new roles and a new consciousness. Soon they too were taking on the character of official representatives of the Church, and imperceptibly the ideals of the monastic priest were projected upon the clerical priest. Not only did he need to be continent, but he was expected to have the ideal of religious consecration as well.

From all of this, a still more complex style began to become dominant: the apostolic-clerical-celibate priest that is basically still with us today. In later centuries, the notions of religious life took on more apostolic and active dimensions, and common life and a seminary experience of religious community became ideals for the clergy. So, our contemporary inheritance is a blend of many diverse styles, purposes and institutions with their necessary confusions, tensions and contradictions. The canonical distinctions between secular and religious clergy and definition of the religious state offer little assistance to separate the tangle.

Today the celibacy of the Catholic priesthood is being widely questioned, yet often enough the questions are posed in semantically meaningless terms. To ask if the "priest" should be celibate is contradictory in itself, since celibacy is part of our very notion of "priest"; what needs to be asked is whether the blending of several institutions over the centuries—each in turn complex and highly evolved—ministry, priesthood, clergy and religious life, into the present canonical institution of the clerical, celibate minister is necessary or necessarily wise.

The commitment to celibacy for the sake of the kingdom of God in its dimension of service and witness is a great and precious gift for the whole church community. Individuals prompted by the Spirit and endowed with this charism may well be selected to preside at the Eucharist and provide other sacramental and magisterial services. But the institutionalized charism of evangelical celibacy is now coming to be more clearly seen as the distinguishing characteristic of religious life, not priesthood as such. The notion of celibacy associated historically with priesthood was more that of cultic purity. In today's post-Freudian world, such a notion has lost much of its meaning.

In the personal development of his vocation, the religious priest first vows to live by the evangelical counsels and then later receives official ministry from the Church. Curiously, the secular priest first is tonsured and received into the clergy, and then, after several minor ministries are given him, he is asked to pledge celibacy as a condition for being ordained for the service of the diocese. The celibacy asked of him is really a defining condition for permanent entrance into the clerical state, and is more for the service of the Church than of the kingdom.

One of the richnesses of the early Church was the great variety of ministries and gifts of the Spirit so widely distributed in the Christian community. However, the increasing concentration of

Christian responsibility over the centuries in the hands of the clergy necessarily limited the development of the apostolate and produced a distorted and truncated style of Christian lay life. One of the aspects of the renewal of the Church in this century has been the rediscovery of the involvement of every one of its members in the one mission. The growing awareness of the common priesthood of all believers forces the ordained priest more and more to seek the meaning of his particular ministry in the service of the many ecclesiastical institutions to which he may be assigned as staff.

There is a considerable difference between the Lord's own institution of a special ministry in the Church in the apostles and the much later development of a clergy. The influence of pagan notions of the sacredness of sacerdotal persons and of the authority of priests in society has very much affected the development of structures of ministry in the Church. Perhaps the real challenge today is not so much to explore the relationships between ministry and celibacy as to liberate both these institutions from the constrictions placed on them by the clerical state. What is at stake is a disestablishment of the Church as a religion, and a reestablishment of its true character and mission as an ordered movement and revolutionary ferment within the larger human society.

There is necessarily a tension in the Church between the demands of the Spirit and the maintenance of the human and institutional forms in which the Church subsists at any moment of history. Certainly this tension exists in the life of the priest. From the moment of his first inclination to priesthood he must assess the requisites of the Church and the promptings of the Spirit, and through the whole of his life this dynamic must inevitably persist. The perennial challenge to the whole Church, to the priesthood and to the individual priest is to maintain a correct balance. There is a need to develop an ideal of priests primarily as men responsive to the Spirit, freely seeking their own fulfilment in loving service. This implies that they will gradually be given the opportunity not only to pursue the kind of ministry that they can best offer but also to choose the style of life—married or celibate for the sake of the kingdom—most suited to their individual personalities, their needs and their vocations.

James E. Dittes

The Symbolic Value of Celibacy for the Catholic Faithful

THEOLOGY, history and Scripture do not provide unambiguous arguments for the obligatory union of priesthood and celibacy, as other papers in this symposium make clear and as pope[1] and synod[2] have acknowledged. Yet priestly celibacy has become a strongly established tradition, and it persists durably. In the face of the uncertain warrants in theology, Scripture and early history, the durability of the tradition becomes something of a puzzle and invites explanation on other grounds. Among these other grounds, some additional understanding of priestly celibacy may come from considering its place in the religious life of the faithful. What does priestly celibacy mean to lay men and women? It is possible that the celibate priesthood, though admittedly not required initially by dogmatic or scriptural considerations, has achieved a central and now indispensable place among the structures which the Church provides to guide the faithful. Has priestly celibacy come to serve an essential function in the spiritual ecology of Catholics which can be tampered with now[3] only at

[1] *Encyclical Letter on Priestly Celibacy* (24 June 1967), especially paragraphs 5, 6, 7, 13.

[2] For example, "The historical concrete realization of every institution within the Church often supposes something more than that which can be deduced abstractly from the Gospel and from dogma." From the statement on celibacy by The World Synod of Bishops, 1971.

[3] At least two different forms of intervention and disruption of the existing spiritual "ecology" need to be considered in asking such questions: (1) the introduction of married priests; (2) the shift of priestly celibacy from the basis that laymen presently perceive as internal voluntary decision to a basis of manifest external obligation. The latter kind of

the risk of the same degree of drastic disruption that is risked by tampering, even by a well-intentioned intervention, with the natural ecology of our environment? Indeed, arguments for priestly celibacy have frequently taken just this turn, and statements by both pope and synod have relied in some substantial part on the analysis that the sheer fact of priestly celibacy exercises a ministry for the faithful, especially as a sign of important transcendent realities.[4]

This paper undertakes to take seriously this possibility, that the celibacy accepted by priests holds an important place in the religious life of the laity. It will explore this hypothesis with the aid of particular psychological tools of analysis. These are by no means the only tools with which to pursue such a question, but they may provide one legitimate approach. In the limited space available, only a point of view can be suggested, *one* way of thinking about celibacy which *may* be useful. There is hardly opportunity here to develop documentation; the validity of such a perspective will have to be tested by the reader in his own reflection on instances of interaction between the celibacy of a priest and the spiritual formation of his people. For the typical Catholic faithful, does his priest's celibacy raise up and respond to important elements in his own religious development?

I. THE AMBIVALENCE OF AWE

When the priestly life is combined with a renunciation of the sexual life, we have brought to stark and compact focus powerful

---

change may be especially crucial in the psychological consideration to follow. It is possible, for example, that some of the psychological arguments about the importance of priestly celibacy in the Church's ministry, arguments on which the papal and synodical statements implicitly rely, are valid only with reference to freely elected celibacy—the impact on the faithful may be the impact of the priest's *choice* of celibacy—whereas these arguments are used to support an obligatory celibacy by priests.

[4] "This continence, therefore, stands as a testimony to the necessary progress of the People of God towards the final goal of their earthly pilgrimage, and as a stimulus for all to raise their eyes to the things above ..." (paragraph 34) is typical of many statements in the papal encyclical, and the Synod writes, "... it is a sign which cannot remain hidden for a long time and which effectively proclaims Christ to men of this time.... The celibate priest signals the presence of the absolute God who invites us to renew ourselves according to his image...."

motives in any person's religious development. The priestly life and the sexual life both evoke profound awe, for both give us intimations of transcendent power and mysterious vitality that they can point to though never contain. But awe is the posture of ambivalence—longing and fear mixed as one. For the sexual life and the priestly life are mixed in their promise, and the powers they point to are too complex to be embraced by simple emotions. In relating to the sexual and the priestly, we blend yearning and avoidance, openness and guardedness, celebration and defilement, reverence and mistrust. We put both the priestly life and the sexual life on special psychological pedestals. In so doing, we elevate and venerate that which we hope may save us. We are also safely distancing ourselves from, even putting into a kind of exile, that which we fear may undo us.

Perhaps more often than not in mankind's religious history, priesthood has been linked with sexuality, occupying the same pedestal and exile. The sexuality linked with priesthood and holiness has tended to be exaggerated, in one direction or another —excessive indulgence as in sacred prostitution and festival orgy, or absolute prohibition as in castration or otherwise zealously enforced virginity. For exaggerated expression is the mark of an ambivalent attitude; and if it is ambivalence/awe that is being expressed in either case, perhaps the apparently opposite expressions—indulgence and prohibition—are representing more nearly similar attitudes than might first appear. Either extreme puts sex —and the priest—on a pedestal, remote from the layman's life and thus simultaneously venerated and mocked.

II. Towards the Priest and the Holy

What does the priest mean to his people? What role does he play in the conscious and unconscious drama of their life development? What place does he occupy in the ecology of their particular life space? As agent of the holy, the priest is the present representative of that domain beyond the horizons of experience from which startling interventions—sometimes benign, sometimes frightening—have come, or been sought. In earlier days, the horizons were narrow, and agents of the domain beyond may have been parents or older brothers and sisters. It was they who seemed able to surprise and startle, to delight or to terrify with powers and gifts delivered from beyond expectation, beyond ken or control. Later on, the horizons may have receded, but a domain of the holy remains beyond them, promising and sometimes delivering the power to change things. Because man can neither well perceive nor predict the ways of the holy—he only knows they are of powerful import to him—he, naturally, does his best to bring the holy under his ken and control. In Christian terms, he replaces the mystery and gift of God's grace with his own faithless and prideful striving for guarantees. Yet the efforts to subdue and control the holy must always be disguised and blended with abject veneration, for the holy must be placated not antagonized and the holy's favour induced by ingratiation as well as by management. Thus, the modern pagan turns to such agents as astrology and drugs, technology and encounter groups as his way of commanding his destiny by capturing and subduing the holy—always with a touch of self-abjection before the holy and its agent mingled with the management of holy and agent by the self. Thus, the Christian is constantly tempted to exploit the truth that God is present in word and sacrament, in Church and priesthood, and to capture God by locking him and his grace into formulas and rituals, by transforming mystery into certainty and grace into guarantee. God is present to the believer through his agents such as Church, word, law, sacrament—and priest— and the posture the believer most naturally takes is to hold the agent, so to speak, in his hand, outstretched and lifted up. This is the posture of devotion and veneration. It is also the posture of controlling and safely distancing. It is man's natural posture towards the holy.

Believers express this attitude towards their priest in many ways. They welcome the priest into their homes and lives; they make him a favourite son, or brother, or uncle, sometimes father; they try to ingratiate themselves with him and to become *his* favourite. Yet he is never quite welcomed unguardedly; they insist on the distinctive title, distinctive dress, distinctive manner in which priest and people relate—even when the priest wants to break down these distancing devices. The laymen confirm the priest's ordination in their own way by daily setting him apart. The priest is "put in his place"—with the fullest ambivalence that expression conveys—by being given the special place in the family living-room or at the speaker's table at the banquet, by getting discounts on trains and exemptions from the army, by being told to stay separate from politics—and from sex. He and the holy are thus honoured by the believers and also thus distanced and controlled.

For the believers match their ambivalence towards the priest and the holy beyond their experience which he represents, with an ambivalence towards these other elements within their experience, perhaps especially towards sex. When the priest is separated from family life, from full individual financial responsibility, from politics and other rights and duties of citizenship—and from sex—one message seems to be: These things in man's daily experience are defiling; the holy must be honoured and not contaminated by them. But there may be another message and perhaps this is the one that the laymen are mostly saying, though unconsciously, when they take the initiative in this separation: There is a vitality to this experience that we want to protect. If the holy can be contained in an absolutely isolated ark, the isolation works both ways; the holy is undefiled by contact from our sordid lives, but our lives, though they feel sordid and empty of grace, also feel rich and full of grace and want to be protected from undue upsetting interference from the domain of the holy. And perhaps there is the further unconscious precaution of aiming to control the holy's agent by depriving him of access to the power we feel surging through family, finances, politics—and sex.

III. AMBIVALENCE AND AWE TOWARDS SEX

Sex stands out among mankind's experiences as especially awesome, especially fraught with mysterious power that both promises healing and fulfilment and also threatens destruction. Because mankind has not yet learned to control and channel this agent, he must keep trying. So men hold the sexual life—just as they hold the priestly life—in the tension of ambivalence, sometimes engaging the experience, but never wholeheartedly and not without a measure of terror and caution, sometimes removing themselves from the experience, but never without a measure of wistfulness and wonder. Humour is a particularly notable expression of ambivalence, simultaneously celebrating and mocking, and the abundance of sexual humour is a measure of the gingerly longing fearful attitude that prevails towards sex. If jokes about psychiatrists are more plentiful these days than jokes about priests, it may be that psychiatrists are perceived more than priests these days as custodians of a mysterious power that must both be captured and fended off. Another way to qualify—as the ambivalence requires—the engagement or the abstention is do it vicariously. The notorious fascination with sex as a "spectator sport" is to be understood just in these terms, a form of measured, carefully guarded involvement. And perhaps celibacy has a similar fascination as a "spectator sport", a measured expression of the separation and control which every person finds necessary in his own relation to sexuality. For the believer to have his priest separated from this powerful element of his own life may, then, be making for him mixed affirmations about sexuality, just as the separation makes mixed affirmations about priesthood. Sexuality is affirmed and preserved from a kind of alien contamination, and protected for himself as a prized possession. But sexuality is also judged as unworthy or defiling or threatening and deserving of exile from the good life.

IV. THE SYMBOLIC MEANING OF PRIESTLY CELIBACY

Taken together, then—and this is the summary of all the preceding paragraphs—priestly celibacy may have this seemingly inconsistent combination of meanings for the layman: (1) priesthood is exalted and sexuality is defiling and to be controlled; (2) sexuality is exalted and priesthood is to be distanced and controlled. The priesthood is too good for sex; and sex is too good for the priest. These two strains are intermingled in the historical and doctrinal arguments in ways that might seem inconsistent unless we realize that they may reflect one or another side of the same ambivalence: celibacy is said to represent a higher order than marriage, a higher order to which the priest properly belongs, representing ties with the absolute God, with the eschaton, with Christ. Yet celibacy is also described dramatically as a sacrifice, as a form of martyrdom, as a kind of price the priest pays for admission to the higher status, rather than as evidence of the status. Sexuality and matrimony can be alluded to, even in successive paragraphs,[5] both as a crippling bondage to be escaped by the priest and also as a great good which is to be sacrificed. Such ambivalence is not at all unusual or improper in religious experience, but it *is* ambivalence.

The priest's celibacy, then, may act out for the layman, in the most concrete and visible form he has available in his experience, important parts of the drama by which he himself comes to terms—a reasonably stable ambivalence *is* a common and successful way of coming to terms—with some very crucial dimensions of his own experience, his own relation with holiness and sexuality. The priest's celibacy affects and resolves crucial motives in the layman's life "vicariously" as does theatre or films or the symbolism of liturgy or the dramatic catharsis of sports events— except that the priest's celibacy is more "real", more permanent and usually more intimately engaging of the layman's life. The priest is more present in his life, than is actor or abstract symbol.

If priestly celibacy did not exist, laymen would have to provide themselves with the equivalent. Indeed, the experience of the Protestants, mostly deprived of a celibate clergy, suggests that this is precisely the case. Protestants tend more vigorously to dehumanize and distance their clergy—charading moralisms, for example, even to the point of hiding liquor or apologizing for profanity in the presence of clergy—in ways that Catholics find unnecessary; if the priest has been separated from sexuality, that is dramatic separation enough. Further, Protestants even tend to deprive their clergy of normal sexuality and family life, in so far as they set artificial and unrealistic norms for the conduct of family life and make excessive dehumanizing and desexualizing demands on the minister's wife. To the degree the minister is perceived as retaining access to the sacred, he is vigorously denied normal family life. These informal but intense restrictions on family relent only as secularization proceeds, and as the minister is taken less seriously in a sacral role.

It might seem that some recent public opinion polls would

[5] For example, paragraphs 28 and 29 of *The Encyclical Letter on Priestly Celibacy* (24 June 1967), but also throughout.

dispute the suggestion here that the lay faithful rely on priestly celibacy to play an important psychic function in their own lives. As many as half or more of those questioned have approved the idea of married clergy. But the single quick poll question is not likely to tap the psychic depth at which the priest's celibacy is involved in the layman's life. Ask the layman to contemplate meeting the priest's wife (the very phrase is provocative enough to have served recently as an intriguing movie title) at the Eucharist, or to consider visiting the couple in the rectory— answers to such questions as these will take longer and be more awkward in forthcoming. The adjustments required to consider assimilating a priest's marriage into our life experience suggest the degree to which his celibacy is lodged in our psychic economy.

V. ASSESSMENT AND ALTERNATIVES

If the priest's celibacy aids lay faithful—some or many—to work through and to establish their own (necessarily persistently ambiguous) relationship with holiness and with sexuality in some way as analysed here, how should this be assessed by a Christian pastoral concern for the welfare of these faithful? Is this a crutch or a ministry? Is this function of the celibacy one that should be regarded as a pre-Christian natural religion which the Christian should be encouraged to mature out of? Or should it be regarded as another means of grace provided through the Church to aid the faithful in their spiritual and moral formation? My personal inclination is towards the latter view—I would suppose that the psychological attempts to specify *how* the priestly celibacy affects the faithful does not make that ministry any less worthy than when it is perceived without such psychological specification. But as a psychologist, I will defer more elaborate assessment of this question to theologians.

However, it does seem important that assessment be made not of priestly celibacy in abstract, but of the actual options that appear to be presently available. It appears that henceforth each layman will experience his priest's marital state in one of these forms:

(1) His priest will be celibate as a personal choice. This corresponds most closely to the situation in the past, which has been

discussed so far in this essay. The legal basis of celibacy has been unclear to the typical layman because never before pressed to public attention, and the layman has most typically regarded his priest as a priest-who-chose-to-be-celibate. The delicate balance of ambivalence which this essay identifies seems to presuppose this personal option, for reasons which can be made more clear below. But we have now seen the end of the ambiguity which permitted the layman to regard the priest more or less as one who had opted for celibacy. The layman is likely to regard his priest's celibacy as he has in the past only if that optionality is now confirmed.

(2) His priest may be married. For those laymen experiencing the kind of psychic needs described above it may be predicted that functional alternatives to the priestly celibacy will be developed. Laymen may imitate their Protestant brethren in finding more subtle ways to deny full sexuality and normal family life to their clergy. It may be that some distinctive elements of Protestant doctrines of God could become more apparent in the attitudes of such Catholics. Protestants have apparently had to distance God—as by emphasizing a stern transcendence—or to control God—tending to make his grace effectively dependent on man's morality or man's subjective "faith"—in ways that Catholics have not found so necessary or congenial. With the holy relatively controlled or distanced through other religious devices, including priestly celibacy, Catholics have thereby been free to achieve a degree of intimacy, or at least immediacy, in their relation with God which might well be envied by many Protestants.

If such alternatives are predictable with respect to means of relating to the holy, so also are alternatives predictable with relation to sexuality; other ways of coming to terms with sexuality may develop, including perhaps a kind of tightness characteristic of some Protestant attitudes. Attitudes towards contraception may be affected, if these are perceived as a way of establishing attitudes towards sexuality; if laymen experience a married priest as a relaxation of restrictions on sexuality, then they might find other restrictions more attractive, as in the form of a ban on contraception. A married priesthood might not be so much the first domino in an assault on sexual morality, as an occasion for bolstering of personal sexual morality, transferring controls from one's priest to oneself.

This suggests that there may be some laymen who have achieved a degree of religious and moral maturity, so that they have found ways of coming to terms with the holy and with sexuality that make unnecessary the role of priestly celibacy that has been described here. For them that celibacy has become a religious vestige whose removal would not upset their psychic ecology and not result in substitute mechanisms.

(3) His priest may be celibate as an act of obedience to law. As the layman would experience it, the priest is celibate because he "must" rather than, as laymen most typically now perceive it, because he "wants" to. This would considerably modify the basis on which the layman relates to his priest's celibacy. It would make changes of two kinds. First, the high visibility of the law would pre-empt and mute the effects of the celibacy. As the law intrudes, like a scrim dropped before the stage, it would separate both priest and people from the meaning of celibacy. If the priest's celibacy is in response largely to the law, then his people will also respond more to the law than to the elements of holiness and sexuality, and the effectiveness of his celibacy for their own lives will be accordingly reduced.

Second, the law would seem to be taking sides in the layman's ambivalence towards the holy and towards sexuality and would have the effect of upsetting the balance that ambivalence had achieved. If the law appears to impose rather visibly heavy restrictions on the holy and on sexuality, the layman is likely to have equally strong psychological need to balance this restriction with a compensating freedom. We predicted above that having a married priest would lead the members of his congregation to find new ways to distance him and to control him and their own sexuality. Here we predict that obviously enforced priestly celibacy will lead the laymen to compensate in the other direction by reducing restrictions on their own sexuality and by reducing the devices for distancing and managing the priest. Laymen, for example, are likely to press for removing the clerical collar and other badges of distinction, and perhaps to press for more lay roles in administration of sacraments and of the institution.

In summary, then, the ministry which the priest's celibacy exercises for his people—as I have tried to discern it here psychologically—seems to presuppose the relatively delicate balance which has been achieved under the circumstances in which people have perceived the celibacy as essentially a choice by the priest. Upsetting this ecological balance—either by inserting a married priesthood or by imposing the celibacy as visibly stern law—is likely to set in motion strong compensating forces, just as any organism mobilizes to resist intrusion and upset. I have tried to predict what some of these reactions would be.

James J. Gill

Psychological Impact of the Change to Optional Celibacy

THE Roman Synod of 1971 is now a matter of history. The atmosphere of expectancy it originally generated has been replaced by a world-wide awareness that the optional celibacy issue is somewhat less urgent and deserves to be approached considerably less emotionally than it was by many just a few months ago. But it is certainly not dead. Questions about the future of celibacy in relationship to diocesan clergy continue to be raised wherever priests, seminarians or laity gather to discuss such topics as new apostolates, experimental life-styles or the shortage of vocations to the priesthood. Moreover, it should not be surprising, I would think, that as long as there remains a deeply rooted drive (or "appetite") thrusting by divine design every adult male's deepest yearnings towards sexual fulfilment and parenthood, there will be wishes expressed by honest men of God that the opportunity to marry and raise a family might become a reality for all priests in the future.

It is more than probable, then, that priests and seminarians will continue during the seasons and years ahead to explore their own convictions, attitudes and desires regarding celibacy, just as they have been doing with increasing freedom and seriousness during the past several years. There is every reason to suspect that sociological surveys will continue to reveal, as they have consistently been disclosing all over the United States, that the majority of priests prefer that celibacy be made optional. It will continue to be dangerous for the Church not to give serious official consideration to these wishes. From a psychological standpoint, either encouraging or permitting persons to explore, identify and express with hopefulness their deepest, long-suppressed or unconsciously repressed yearnings is a potentially explosive deed. If the Church goes on failing to react to these wishes, or frustrates them in an insensitive or callous way, it will run the risk of having to deal ultimately with an intense and widespread build-up of anger, resentment and even rejection of the priestly career. It is unfortunate that the Church's official response to the needs and wishes of a large proportion of dedicated and active priests has been, even in the forum provided by the Synod, alarmingly inadequate. Still, it may be a fortunate thing that so far there has been no change in the celibacy requirement, since behind most changes, including the one the majority of priests in America are requesting, there lies a potential threat to human nature.

Life involves a series of major and minor adjustments, some made consciously and others unconsciously, which help us to remain in psychological equilibrium with our environment, including people, the locale, our work and ordinary daily events. In other words, we tend naturally to react to changes in ways that are technically called "ego-adaptive". Behind almost every change that occurs in our lives, there is a possible emotional trauma which could steal away our peace of mind. It springs from the fact that change generally takes something from us and replaces it with something not yet experienced. What we are being called upon to surrender is usually an element of the surrounding "reality" to which we have struggled to adjust. We find ourselves all too often unsure that we will be able to cope as successfully with the new person, situations or events about to enter our lives. This uncertainty commonly expresses itself in the vague, unpleasant, more or less intense feeling we call "anxiety"—one which deserves the place it holds in the psychologist's catalogue of "distressful or painful emotions".

On the other hand, Ben Jonson tells us that "No one is happy but by the anticipation of change. The change itself is nothing. It is only followed by the desire to change again." One might wonder how he could believe this, since change involves the potential for generating as distressful an experience as the kind just mentioned. I would suggest that the apparent contradiction might be resolved by recalling the fact that, in instances of change, it makes a great deal of difference *who* is taking the initiative. Pain most often comes to the one who is passive, resistant and acted upon. Pleasure and satisfaction predictably accrue to the innovator who has a positive attitude towards the good being sought through the change.

All of which brings us to the predictable future change from mandatory to optional celibacy. Such a change will undoubtedly bring satisfaction to many and distress to others; this is inevitable. It will surely have a significant impact on such diverse issues as the perseverance of priests, the fidelity of the laity, the recruitment of seminarians, the government of the Church, the provision of ecclesiastical services, the image of the Roman Catholic Church in the eyes of non-members, and the mode of preparing candidates for the priestly career—to mention only a few of the *foci* where important reverberations will unquestionably occur. Prescinding from the favourable response that will come from those priests who have already declared a preference for optional celibacy, there will be others who will be neutral to the change, some who will be ambivalent towards it, and a number (not by any means *negligible*) who will view it negatively.

Priests who are reasonably satisfied with the celibate state or consider themselves already too old for marriage will accept the change and adjust to it compliantly, as long as these are individuals who remain tolerant of the wishes and choices of others, and at the same time flexible in adjusting to new realities. However, for a variety of reasons (some of which are quite complex) other priests will respond by experiencing a state of more or less severe emotional distress. Some will even protest, I would expect, by angrily separating themselves from active duty in the priesthood.

Why such negative reactions? Because the attitude of a large number of priests towards celibacy as an inseparable element within the Western priesthood serving for them what is technically termed an "ego-defensive" function.[1] These men are likely to support their resistance to a change in the celibacy requirement

---

[1] Unconsciously operating processes by which a person can protect himself from anxiety arising from his own unacceptable impulses or inclinations—as well as from some threatening forces outside himself—are known as "ego-defensive mechanisms".

by appealing tenaciously to some willowy line of theological reasoning or "evidence" drawn from personal or vicarious experience. On the occasion of this change, these men will have to begin to deal (at a deep level within each individual's personality) with anxiety regarding their own masculinity. New socio-sexual pressures will provoke and increase an inner tension which will be emotionally painful for these priests. While decrying the Church's permissiveness, they will be experiencing the loss of one of their best sources of protection—one that has enabled them to avoid facing their own arrested personality development and resulting psycho-sexual immaturity. The geographical proximity of married priests, added to the public attention suddenly focused on their own sexuality, will seriously threaten these vulnerable men psychologically. They may find excuses to flee the situation causing them discomfort (while blaming the hierarchy who authorize the change), or they may—if their emotional problem becomes very painful—require psychotherapeutic assistance to facilitate their adjustment. But I do not mean to state that all of those who are disturbed this way will react so dramatically. Most of these men, if they "work their problem through" (either interpersonally by means of social contact with women, or in therapy), will discover that they are merely harbouring long-standing and' deep fears of sexual inadequacy and are not in fact as incapable as they suspect in regard to functioning successfully in a heterosexual manner.

There are other priests who also feel strongly positive towards mandatory celibacy whose attitude is serving what is called a "value-expressive" function. Unlike the defensive attitude mentioned above (which prevents the individual from revealing to himself, as well as to others, his deep-seated sexual problem), this healthier kind of attitude enables a man to give positive expression to one of his profound (or "central") values and to the type of person he conceives himself to be. The Catholic clergyman whose celibate style of life reflects his cherished beliefs and an accurately formed self-image generally derives considerable personal satisfaction from his unmarried priesthood. There will be many such men who will not be distressed over change in the Church's discipline with regard to celibacy. However, there is a type of individual who employs his conscience (or "super-ego") not only as a means of guiding his own personal functioning (in conformity with his "ego-ideal") but acts as conscience for his peers, requiring that they too live up to *his* standards. This is a man whose nature tends irrationally to insist that others be bound by the same laws which restrict his own behaviour, even though his obligations have been assumed through a personal or voluntary choice. He is troubled emotionally by the proximity of others who are enjoying the expression of an inclination he has deliberately blocked within himself. Such a man is found relatively frequently among Catholic priests, particularly in those who manifestly reflect attitudes towards others that deserve to be branded as "moralistic". When the change regarding celibacy occurs, these men—if they opt to remain unmarried—will be inclined to be angry and punitive towards those who take advantage of the opportunity to express their sexuality maritally.

Just in passing it seems worth noting that both the ego-defensive and the value-expressive attitudes towards maintenance of the celibacy requirement have at least one thing in common; they are in favour of maintaining the *status quo*. It might be helpful, in view of this fact, to recall that this is simply one of countless possible examples which reveal that different people develop similar attitudes towards the same object, person or situation for *different reasons*. This truth deserves to be recalled when one is attempting to achieve a change of attitude within the several types of individuals already discussed. A general principle applicable to the changing of attitudes is this: the grounds on which an object has attained a certain degree of centrality for a given individual should be the target towards which new, persuasive and relevant information is aimed in an attempt to change his attitude towards that object. An uncomplicated example of this sort of *aiming* would be a person's describing a lengthy series of successful marriages begun after men had reached the age of forty-five, in an effort to change a listening priest's positive attitude towards the celibacy requirement if he has built it on a bedrock assumption that men in their mid-forties are too old to marry.

A positive disposition towards the Church's current celibacy situation can arise from yet another source. In the psychology of a number of priests, their attitude serves what is called an "adjustment function". This sort of psychic manoeuvring is seen in a person's striving to maximize the rewards in his external environment and minimize the penalties he must pay. He forms attitudes which are dependent on his present or past perceptions of the utility of the attitudinal object for him. Thus, a priest may have found his life free from the ordinary stresses and worries that are prominent in the adult lives of most married men whose wives and children naturally make continuous demands upon them. A strongly positive attitude towards the value of celibacy may be this type of priest's principal means of maintaining his desired goal (a relatively worry-free existence), and the easiest way for him to avoid the undesirable situation which would result if he were to have a wife and children perennially and heavily dependent upon him.

For the sake of completeness, perhaps mention should be made briefly of the resentment that a celibacy law change will naturally generate in the hearts of some older priests who have been obliged to forgo, at the cost of considerable (and sometimes *inconceivable*) pain, the gratifications of marriage, home and family they have through many long and lonesome years fantasized and desired. These men will be understandably angry over the fact that younger men are to be granted the joys and pleasures they themselves have been forbidden.

Among the Catholic laity, reactions to a change in the discipline regarding clerical celibacy will be as varied as those of priests. Some will rejoice over the fact that their clergyman is now being recognized as "human"—having feelings and needs and yearnings like the rest of men. Some will remain *indifferent*; which is simply stating that whether the priest is free to marry, actually marries, is required to remain celibate, or prefers to do so, his personal status will make virtually no difference at all to them. Others will be *ambivalent*, perceiving some potential gain for themselves along with some degree of personal loss as entailed in the shift. There are also many Catholics who have felt that previous changes in the Church's externals and discipline (for example, those affecting liturgy, the presence of statues in churches, the manner of administering the sacraments, or the official list of saints) have tested their faith about as far as it can be stretched. They have been wondering: *"What will go next?" "Will there be anything left in the long run in which I will be able to believe?"*

Previously educated to view the Church as unchangeable in creed, code and cult, countless individuals have been traumatized by the rapid series of changes effected since Vatican II, and they have not yet been able to adjust to the fact that even further changes (including some that will radically affect their lives) are bound to occur. There is recent statistical evidence, however, that most of the laity in the United States are beginning to hear the message that a change in the Church's celibacy situation is a definite possibility.

There are some people who are pessimistic about any and every change. They anticipate finding that every gain achieved through change will be outweighed by the loss they will experience. Some, in *paranoid* fashion, will consider changes—particularly the abruptly executed ones—as results of the machinations of self-seeking and destructive individuals dedicated to harming or annoying them. But those who will react to a celibacy change in a way that demands and deserves the closest possible attention are the multitude of Catholics who have formed towards the unmarried priest a set of attitudes that are unrealistic and based on child-like wishes and fantasy.

Every child forms in his mind a picture of what he imagines to be the qualities of an ideal father. Most of these attributes are derived from his impressions of his own father as the child experiences or wishes him to be. The characteristics included are often exaggerated, unattainable or even contradictory, and they are calculated to meet the infantile needs or yearnings of the child. The "good father" is conceived by children as being always readily available, holding no preference for anyone ahead of them, not having a prior commitment to anyone other than them; he is also omnipotent, omniscient, not sexually demanding, free from preoccupations and problems of his own, unambitious for himself, omnicompetent, requiring nothing from them emotionally or financially, and working more for them than for himself; furthermore, they see him as dedicated to fulfilling their wishes and desires as well as to meeting all their needs, and capable of allowing them to depend upon him almost entirely for all their most fundamental necessities. Unfortunately, there is ample evidence that there are innumerable Catholics who have carried (unconsciously) a "good father" image like this into their adult lives and projected it upon their father-priest. It will be difficult for them to face the "realities" about him (for example, his family obligations, sexuality, limited availability, economic needs) when his marital status demands that they do so.[2] It is regrettable that many priests in many ways still behave in such a manner that unrealistic expectations on the part of members of the laity are perpetuated. There is already need for the development of a new image of "a priest" as a growing, limited, professional, charitable and committed *human* being. Such an image will not be generated in an instant; nor can it afford to be neglected until the celibacy law is abrogated.

The priest with a wife and children to present to his parishioners will be in need of a new mode of social response. Not only will Catholics be called upon financially to support this extra burden, but many will experience a profound sense of personal loss, since they formerly considered the priest as belonging in a special way to *them*, not only for theological reasons but because he was single and available.[3] We will see, too, a tendency on the part of parishioners, particularly women, to reject the priest's wife as a competitor. The emotional problems of a clergyman's wife and children in relation to gaining parochial acceptance are already well documented by psychiatrists and familiar in Protestant circles. Priests who will be permitted to marry will have to become familiar with such "facts of life" and in justice acquaint their prospective brides with them.

Another reality the married priest will have to face is the abrupt loss of status he will experience when many Catholics come to view him as no longer undertaking the "heroic" through a life of celibacy, but instead seeking an "ordinary" mundane existence like their own. Our human nature looks among our fellow men for models who will display exceptional competence or virtue. The remarkable achievements of *others* (technical as well as moral) contribute more to the development and maintenance of

[2] Even adult Protestants often find it difficult to think realistically about their married ministers. I have heard a number of women state how impossible it is for them to accept the fact that their clergyman regularly has sexual relations with his wife.

[3] This inclination to "adopt" the bachelor has been portrayed with deep and clever insight during the past several years by S. Sondheim in his brilliant Broadway musical *Company*.

our sense of personal worth and hopefulness than most individuals suspect. The poet's veneration of the Virgin Mary as "our tainted nature's solitary boast" casts a hint in the direction of this fact. But when Roman Catholic priests are no longer required to demonstrate throughout their lives the highly symbolic and challenging charism of celibacy, there is likely to be felt by many Christians a *sense of loss* that will be based on the dynamic just mentioned but which most will find hard to explain.

Some people will regard the priest who marries as one who is letting them down, or as another weakened god who is revealing his feet of clay. Even those priests who do not themselves choose to marry will have to be prepared to deal with these reactions which will reveal a change of attitude on the part of many of the laity towards priests in general. Priests and seminarians should be provided with carefully and thoroughly prepared materials which will assist them to face realistically and cope with the variety of responses that will come from the laity when the celibacy option becomes available. Some expert social psychologists should begin to prepare such presentations as soon as feasible. Even the publicity currently being given priests' desires regarding freedom to marry is changing the attitude of many towards the Catholic clergy. Laymen increasingly complain: "Priests have become self-preoccupied, not concerned about us any longer." We also hear nearly as frequently: "These senates and other groups of priests are just trying to make the priest's life *easier*; they think marriage would do that for them."

Those who remain active as priests but do not take advantage of the opportunity to marry will require even greater emotional support from fellow clergymen and laity than most are currently receiving. We might expect that many small communities of celibate diocesan priests would be formed, since the human need for sharing life will insist on finding a substitute for the rectory-type existence that will vanish when the ranks of single priests are gradually thinned by marriage. With less stringent regulations affecting the social behaviour of the Catholic clergy, closer spiritual direction or counselling will have to be provided, so that each celibate priest will have the opportunity to discuss frequently his attitudes, convictions, feelings and behaviour with a fellow priest who is experienced and competent as a facilitator of spiritual and moral growth.[4]

The assignments given to celibate priests will have to be selected carefully. These men will need to be protected from inheriting the difficult, precarious and less attractive jobs which their family-obligated confrères must turn down. Their assigned work will have to be personally gratifying enough to provoke the feelings of justifiable pride and self-fulfilment that will enable these men to persevere. In the past we have lost too many celibate priests who complained that they felt unfulfilled in their work, and as a result frustrated, unchallenged and lonely. The salary of a celibate should be equitable in comparison with that paid to the married priest. But he will have to be spiritually formed in such a way that economic affluence does not deprive him of the poverty of spirit his Christlike vocation enjoins. Bishops will have to refrain from overworking the celibate members of the clergy and from giving them the more demanding and less rewarding responsibilities "because they are not tied down with families". We might expect that candidates for the priesthood who want to remain celibate will find their way in larger numbers into religious orders, and that some who are ordained and wish to remain celibate will become affiliated with new religious congregations of men and women (married as well as single) living communally.

It seems obvious that it would be advisable for the change in the celibacy situation to take place *gradually*. The Church will need to discover which parishes will be ready to support married priests and their families. Many among the clergy and laity will require considerable time and the accumulation of convincing evidence in order to bring about a change in attitude to the relationship between priesthood and celibacy. Any attitude is generally altered most effectively by considering information which casts new light on the object of the attitude, so those who have a negative attitude in this instance will have to be shown that the married priest is at least as successful in ministry as the celibate. They will also have to be persuaded that the Church and they themselves are not losing more than they are gaining as a result

---

[4] I would think that members of religious orders of priests might increasingly specialize in this ministry of counselling.

of this change. Recalling the fact that people resist change when they anticipate deprivation and regard the change as being *inflicted* upon them, I would suggest that the shift to optional celibacy should be presented as being for the benefit of the Church, not just for marriage-seeking priests. It should also be made as clear as possible that this change is certainly not being imposed on or adopted against anyone. Even so, any parishioner whose habitual style of thinking happened to be paranoid will probably interpret it as a plot instigated (probably by Communists) to corrupt the Holy Church.

But how can evidence be provided which will ultimately prove convincing and thus accomplish a change in the attitudes of those who are now negative towards optional celibacy? I would think that a limited number of married priests could be observed rather closely in some part of the world that is ready for this experiment, perhaps where the faithful are many but priests are few. It would be possible to prepare for ordination a number of men who are already married, or to allow ordained priests or seminarians to marry. But if such a plan were followed it would be difficult to limit the marriages that would in all probability be initiated and the dating that would begin in all parts of the world. Many priests and seminarians would feel *entitled* to date and marry and would have difficulty respecting any territorial limits set down. The appearance of arbitrariness which generates a spirit of resentment and rebellion would have to be avoided in setting up such an experiment. Fixing a cut-off point related to age, years in the priesthood, or any similar factor, would undoubtedly prove as unsatisfactory as allowing ordained priests to marry only within certain territorial areas.

It would seem *least* provocative of emotional distress among the clergy for men already married to join the ranks of priests in areas where there is urgent need for more ministers. The success they achieved in combining marriage with ministry could be reported to clergy and laity around the world more completely than the way in which the experiments of "worker-priest" were reviewed year by year in Europe a few decades ago. The experiment could continue until the climate of acceptance became right for the change to take place in other parts of the world. Seminarians everywhere would have the opportunity to develop a new attitude towards the priesthood and to look ahead to the possibility of marrying, if they should so choose. Their psycho-sexual development would be facilitated through opportunities to date young women. It could be understood that they would not be ordained if they were to marry before completing their theological studies, the way midshipmen in the Navy and air force cadets have been refused authorization to marry as long as they remain in a state of preparation for commissioning. But if a seminarian were to decide to marry, he could finish his theological studies, then wait to be ordained until official approval of a married priesthood is granted. The same discipline could prevail for men already ordained who have married or wish to marry. They, too, could function in some useful but limited way ministerially until the period of experimentation is over and the option to marry has been authorized for all.

For the well-being of the Church it will be extremely important for the priests and seminarians who eventually choose to marry to make a success of their marriages. This might be expected to occur with predictable regularity as long as these men and their wives are individuals who have reached *maturity* in psycho-sexual growth. Consequently, it will be essential for faculties of seminaries to learn to provide or facilitate the various types of emotional experience that will help future priests to attain the highest level of psychological and social development possible for them. The recommendations made by Eugene Kennedy and Victor Heckler in *The Loyola Psychological Study of the Ministry and Life of the American Priest* (1971) should prove to be of considerable value in specifying the aims and quality of these experiences.

I would like to conclude by presenting, in skeletal fashion, a few basic principles borrowed from the discipline of social psychology, which might be profitably kept in mind during consideration of ways in which attitudes towards the celibacy requirement can be changed. I will simply list them and occasionally make reference to the specific issue under discussion here:

1. Attitude change depends generally on the receipt of new information that is in some way relevant to the attitude object (optional celibacy) from the point of view of the attitude holder.

2 When an attitude shifts, this does not usually occur because of any gross alteration of feeling towards the property (celibacy) in itself. Instead, another property (marriage and parenthood) of great subjective importance and with a positive valence has been introduced.

3. The cognitive content of the object changes first, then the affective change follows.

4. The majority of attitude changes towards an object occur because the object has in fact changed its properties. (Hence, people who are opposed to linking optional celibacy with priesthood are more likely to accept this when they see it as a *de facto* situation than they are likely to change their attitude towards it because of rational argument or persuasion.)

5. Attitudes towards an object are more easily changed, all other things being equal, if the object is less firmly embedded in some means-end chain that is important to the individual than it is when it lies in a more central position. (Hence, the laity may well be more susceptible to an attitude change towards celibacy than the pastor who fears being abandoned by his assistant, or the bishop who sees his priests about to become fully self-supporting.)

6. (Stated earlier in this article.) The grounds on which an object has attained a certain degree of centrality for a given individual should be the target at which new, persuasive and relevant information is aimed in an attempt to change his attitude to that object.

7. Deep personal experience with the attitude object is a most potent setting for attitude change when the initial attitude is based on a misperception or inadequate information.

8. Information communicated by persuasion differs from that which would be conveyed by direct transactions with the object itself. Direct information is usually more persuasive than socially mediated information.

9. Evaluation of the source of information affects the evaluation of the persuasive message, and this influences the likelihood of attitudinal change.

10. Although a source cannot deny that his attitude differs from that of his listener with respect to the object of persuasion, he can help to minimize the listener's sense of attitudinal

distance from him by making clear to the listener that they hold very similar positions in terms of other attitudes, even ones that are quite irrelevant to the object of persuasion.

11. Individuals are less responsive to a persuasive message if they expect in advance to disagree with it than they are to the same message when not forewarned.

12. The listener is least likely to feel that the source has any persuasive intent towards him when the message is not even addressed to him in the first place, as is the case with overheard conversations.[5]

[5] See, for example, Chapter 4, "Attitude Change", in *Social Psychology*, by Newcombe, Turner and Converse (New York, 1965).

James A. Coriden

Celibacy, Canon Law and Synod 1971

IN ORDER to reach some understanding of the celibacy question from the point of view of church discipline, it will be helpful (1) to review the debate and decision of the synod in the context of what went before, (2) to sketch the present law on celibacy, its origins and the values it was intended to preserve, and (3) recommend some possible courses of action for the future.

I. THE DECISION OF THE SYNOD OF BISHOPS

The synod of bishops resoundingly declared that "the law of priestly celibacy existing in the Latin Church is to be kept in its entirety". A majority of the synod of fathers also opposed the priestly ordination of married men. Pope Paul confirmed these positions on 30 November 1971.[1]

What was the background for these decisions? What events led up to them?

The Second Vatican Council, in a brief statement in 1965, approved and confirmed the law of celibacy for those called to the priesthood in the Latin Church.[2] This was done without the benefit of debate or extended exchange because Pope Paul, as in the case of birth control, pre-empted the issue. In a letter read to the Council on 11 October 1965, the Pope cautioned against a public discussion of the matter, expressed his intention to maintain the

[1] The documents of the Synod are found in A.A.S., 63 (1972) 897 ff.
[2] *Decree on Ministry and Life of Priests*, art. 16.

ancient law, and promised to strengthen its observance by setting forth the values and reasons for the suitability of the law.[3]

The short statement which issued from the Council, although it was not the result of the full conciliar process, did clarify some important points: (a) it declared that continence is not demanded by the very nature of the priesthood (and it expressed esteem and support for the different tradition of the Eastern Churches; (b) it stated that the source of the obligation of celibacy is ecclesiastical law, thus laying to rest the theory of the "implicit vow" which had been held by many influential authors;[4] (c) it refrained from basing the discipline on motives of "cultic purity" or a depreciation of marriage and sexuality; rather it gave positive theological, spiritual and pastoral reasons for priestly celibacy (e.g., undivided devotion to Christ, dedication to the apostolic task, a sign of the world to come).

The Pope's own elaborate and heartfelt letter on priestly celibacy was issued on 24 June 1967.[5] The encyclical set forth at some length the arguments alleged for changing the present discipline, solemnly reaffirmed the law ("... we consider that the present law of celibacy should today continue to be firmly linked to the priestly ministry"[6]), and expounded the reasons for it (christological, ecclesiological and eschatological) together with pastoral admonitions and encouragement.

Although widely distributed and commented upon, the encyclical did not terminate the "celibacy debate" on either the popular or theological level. Indeed, the literature generated by this sensitive issue was prodigious and impressive.[7] An astonishing number of serious authors addressed themselves to the ques-

---

[3] H. Vorgrimler, *Commentary on Documents of Vatican* II, vol. 4, pp. 200 and 282.

[4] E.g., Bertrams, Bouscaren, Wernz, Vermeersch. Some canonists now contend that sacred orders cannot be a diriment impediment to marriage. The *Constitution on the Church in the Modern World*, art. 26, affirmed that the right to found a family is inviolable. Such a fundamental human right must not be denied by positive law. It must remain within the disposition of the person.

[5] *Sacerdotalis Caelibatus*, A.A.S., 59 (1967) 657ss.

[6] *Ibid.*, p. 662.

[7] E.g., the *Bibliographie internationale sur le sacerdoce et le ministère 1969*, published by the Centre de Documentation (Montreal, 1971), contains almost four hundred pages and lists nearly seven thousand items.

tion in the last five years. Journalists, columnists and opinion samplers added to the discussion and made the topic familiar to all. Several episcopal conferences issued formal statements in support of the discipline of celibacy.[8] Resolutions passed by priests' groups and surveys of the attitudes and opinions of priests and laity revealed quite different views.

The recommendations of the Dutch Pastoral Council in January 1970 highlighted and accentuated these divergent opinions on celibacy. The Dutch assembly resolved by overwhelming votes: that the obligation of celibacy as a condition for the fulfilling of priestly ministry be abolished; that celibacy no longer be a condition for entering the priesthood; that priests who have married be readmitted to the priesthood; that priests who desire to marry should be allowed to continue to function as priests; and that married men should be admitted to the priesthood.[9]

These startling and radical requests from the Church of Holland occasioned a pained and forceful letter from Pope Paul to Cardinal Villot, his Secretary of State, reasserting strongly the traditional connection between celibacy and priesthood.[10] In the context of this firm rejection of the Dutch resolutions, however, the Pope asked whether mature married men should not be ordained to the priesthood in areas where there is an extreme shortage of priests. He said that this possibility deserved serious study since it would have implications for the universal Church.

The ministerial priesthood and justice in the world were announced as the two topics for consideration of the episcopal synod of 1971. As preparations for the event advanced, the debate over the celibacy issue intensified. In October 1970 the International Commission of Theologians released a "working paper" on priestly ministry[11] which, after a thorough and profound examination of ministry in the Church, extolled the values of priestly celibacy, but also expressed an openness to the ordination of married men where that was seen to benefit the preaching of the Gospel. It did not recommend the continuance in ministry of priests who marry. This report was intended for transmission to

[8] E.g., in France, Germany and the United States in 1969.
[9] *National Catholic Reporter*, 14 January 1970.
[10] A.A.S., 62 (1970) 98ss.
[11] *Le Ministère Sacerdotal* (Paris, 1971), pp. 100–13.

the synod of bishops, but it was apparently not made available until late in the spring of 1971.

On 15 February 1971, the synod secretariat sent to the episcopal conferences of the world a preliminary schema (*Lineamenta Argumentorum de Quibus Disceptabitur*) on the ministerial priesthood.[12] In its treatment of the relation between the priesthood and celibacy the document laid heavy emphasis on the appropriateness of the present discipline. It raised the question of the eventual ordination of married men in the same cautious tones and with the same limiting conditions that Pope Paul used in his letter to Cardinal Villot.

Episcopal conferences meeting in all parts of the world during the spring and summer of 1971 discussed the problems of the priesthood, including the issue of celibacy as they selected and "instructed" their delegates to the synod. Priests' groups met during the same period, and many went on record favouring a change to optional celibacy.[13] A major study of United States priests, sponsored by the bishops and released in the spring, reported that a majority favoured a change in the law of celibacy and a large majority expected such a change to take place, even though the priests saw positive values for ministry in their own celibate lives.[14] A careful survey of Canadian priests, reported in June 1971, indicated that a clear majority were in favour of optional celibacy for priests. A majority felt that change will come and the overwhelming majority favoured the ordination of married men.[15] A nation-wide opinion poll, taken in the U.S. in June 1971, showed a majority of Catholics in favour of allowing priests to marry and continue to function as priests.[16]

[12] *De Sacerdotio Ministeriali* (In Civitate Vaticana: Typis Polyglottis Vaticanis, 1971), pp. 6, 19–20, 36–8.
[13] E.g., this statement passed by a vote of 193 to 18 at the March 1971 meeting of the National Federation of Priests' Councils in the U.S.: "We ask that the choice between celibacy and marriage for priests now active in the ministry be allowed and that the change begin immediately." *America*, 3 April 1971, p. 341.
[14] *Study on Priestly Life and Ministry* (Washington, D.C.; National Conference of Catholic Bishops, 1971), pp. 24–69.
[15] *A Working Paper on The Ministerial Priesthood in Preparation for Synod 1971* (Ottawa; Canadian Catholic Conference, 1971), pp. 54–5, 121–33.
[16] Gallup Organization survey taken 23–8 June 1971.

Shortly before the synod began Pope Paul ordered copies of a book defending priestly celibacy sent to all the delegates. The book, *Sacerdoce et celibat*, edited at Louvain by Joseph Coppens,[17] is a massive compilation of articles and documentation which support the historical and theological link between celibacy and priesthood. It was quickly translated into several languages.

It was perhaps the animated exchange over priestly celibacy more than any other single problem which caused the Pope solemnly to caution the synod fathers against the dangerous pressures which surrounded their gathering.[18] He addressed this admonition to the two hundred and ten assembled bishops[19] at the opening Mass on 30 September 1971.

The first item on the synod agenda was the question of the ministerial priesthood. Discussions on the doctrinal principles of the priesthood occupied the first week of the synod in both general sessions and in twelve lingual groups (wherein a few priest auditors were able to intervene). When the celibacy issue was touched upon in these more theological talks, the feeling was for maintaining the discipline of priestly celibacy as it is and for presenting more convincingly the manifold suitability of the celibate state for the ministry of priests.[20]

The practical problems of the priesthood occupied the efforts of the synod fathers from the introductory statement of Cardinal Enrique y Tarancon (Toledo) on Thursday, 7 October, until Tuesday, 19 October. There were a hundred and thirty-two interventions in general sessions, besides the reports of the lingual groups which met several times in that period. Many other issues related to the life and work of priests were treated, e.g., pastoral planning, the relationship between the bishop and his priests, temporal occupations and political involvements, economic needs, spiritual life, ordination of women, etc., but the present law of

[17] (Gembloux–Louvain, 1971), 752 pages.
[18] A.A.S., 63 (1971) 770.
[19] Of this total a hundred and forty-three were the elected representatives of episcopal conferences, another twenty per cent were selected by the pope, fifty per cent of the total number were from the third world; the average age of the synod fathers was fifty-eight.
[20] Sources for this account of synodal activities include: N.C. News Service daily reports, correspondents' reports of Associated Press, *Washington Post, New York Times*, and *National Catholic Reporter, La Civiltà Cattolica, America*, other journals, and personal conversations.

celibacy of priests and the possibility of ordaining married men received major attention (at least a hundred interventions touched on it).

Since many of the bishops' talks were in reaction to Cardinal Enrique y Tarancon's opening message, it is useful to repeat his remarks on this point:

The Priesthood and Celibacy

Surveys that have been carried out show that this is not a central problem. Nor is it so vast as some people think. It has to be faced, however, with absolute loyalty and calmness. Whatever may be the decision the Church will come to in this matter, it will not bear fruit if the evangelical and pastoral motives behind it are not properly understood and evaluated. Here are some reflections:

(i) Nobody doubts that celibacy is a legitimate form of life that can be lived humanly in the Christian spirit. The motive of love that inspires it should penetrate all aspects of the person's life.

(ii) The priestly ministry brings with it a fittingness for the complete availability of the priest for his priestly tasks in the service of his fellow men and of the Church.

(iii) When the Church demands the charism of celibacy, she does not do so for reasons of "ritualistic purity". Nor does she consider that this is the way for achieving sanctity. Her intention is above all to find the best way in which the priestly ministry can be exercised within the community for the building up of the Church.

(iv) Celibacy is still a valid sign when it is not lived in a mere legalistic way. It is a mysterious witness of love for the Kingdom of God.

(v) This charism, however, cannot be assured for an individual by the Church even through the administration of sacraments. It presupposes a life of strong faith.

(vi) Before the step is taken of ordaining married men for pastoral necessity, the whole concept of pastoral action has to be carefully examined. It means the possibility of a better distribution of ministries, in which deacons and the laity could assume certain functions.

(vii) The training of candidates for the celibate priesthood must be enriched with theological, spiritual and philosophical thought.[21]

Considering the wide diversity of opinion in the Church before the synod, the unanimity of the bishops at the synod was truly remarkable. The reaffirmation of the law of celibacy for all those seeking ordination or presently in priestly ministry was nearly without dissent. Not one of the lingual groups voted against the discipline of celibacy, and the votes were not even close. Bishop John Gran (Oslo) was the only speaker who openly favoured "optional celibacy". Bishop Alexander Carter (Sault Ste Marie), speaking for the Canadian hierarchy, asked for the ordination of married men and the readmission to ministry of priests who had married, but was opposed to ordaining single men who were uncommitted to celibacy and to permitting the option of marriage to those already ordained. In fact, an overview of the interventions indicates that the possibility of marriage for those already ordained priests was never seriously considered at the synod. All efforts were directed towards reasserting the present discipline, purifying and clarifying the theological and pastoral motives for celibacy, and restating them as firmly and persuasively as possible.

The ordination of mature married men was, on the other hand, a serious issue and one which found the fathers sharply divided. After the first few days of discussion, several observers were predicting that this innovation would almost certainly be approved. Some say that it was the fearful admonitions of Cardinal William Conway (Armagh) and others on 12 October which stemmed the tide. They warned that the smallest breach in the rule of celibacy would soon result in its destruction.

Those who favoured the possibility of ordaining married men were split on the authority question. Should the authorization be reserved to the Pope or should the episcopal conferences be allowed to permit it? Cardinal Leo Suenens (Malines-Brussels) spoke strongly for the responsibility of local hierarchies to provide for the pastoral care of their people. The majority was clearly in the opposite direction; they wanted no part of the decision on

[21] N.C. News Service foreign report for 8 October 1971, pp. 3-4.

the national level. In fact, the final vote indicates that the majority of synod fathers were opposed to any ordination of married men at all; they simply did not want to repudiate what the popes had already permitted on several occasions, namely, the ordination of married men (usually Protestant ministers or Anglican priests who had joined the Roman Catholic communion) in exceptional circumstances. However, the division of feeling on this issue continued to the end of the synod. The vote on 5 November, the day before adjournment, showed that about forty-five per cent of the members were not opposed to the ordination of mature married men where pastoral needs called for it; they preferred to leave the decision to the Pope.

Pope Paul's closing remarks to the synod, in tones of gratitude and relief, singled out for particular mention the bishops' re-affirmation of the law of celibacy as stated in the Second Vatican Council. He hastened to add his own confirmation of that decision.[22] Again in his terse rescript accepting, confirming and making public the two synodal documents ("The Ministerial Priesthood" and "Justice in the World") he drew special attention to only one item: "that in the Latin Church there shall continue to be observed in its entirety with God's help, the present discipline of priestly celibacy".[23]

II. The Present Law and Its Origins

What exactly is the present law which imposes the obligation of celibacy on priests, and what were the circumstances which gave rise to it? The answer to this twofold question is well known to canonists and historians, but many, including priests and theologians, tend to assume that the law always existed and that the same reasons were always given for it. A brief, factual summary may dispel some of these misconceptions.

The heart of the matter is Canon 132, par. 1, of the Code of Canon Law (a. 1918): "Clerics in major orders (subdiaconate, diaconate, priesthood) are prevented from marrying and are so obliged to observe chastity that those sinning against it are also guilty of sacrilege. . . ." This principal legislation is supported by several related rules, namely:

[22] A.A.S., 63 (1971) 833.   [23] *Ibid.*, p. 897.

—that a married man who receives major orders without a dispensation, even though in good faith (e.g., presuming his wife has died), is forbidden to exercise the orders;[24]

—that clerics must be careful not to have in their houses nor to associate habitually with women who might be objects of suspicion;[25]

—that the bishop is to judge when such associations may be a scandal or a danger of incontinence, and he may forbid them; those disregarding his prohibitions are presumed to be living in concubinage and may be suspended and deprived of income;[26]

—that clerics in sacred orders attempt marriage invalidly, and those attempting marriage even civilly are *ipso facto* excommunicated and are impeded from exercising their orders or receiving further orders;[27]

—that ordinations validly received never become void, and even when one in major orders is "reduced to the lay state" he is still obliged to celibacy until dispensed from that specific obligation by papal authority;[28]

—that procedures for reduction to the lay state and for dispensation from the obligations of priestly office are lengthy and detailed; once dispensed the priest is still subject to limitations, e.g., leaving the area where he is known, marrying very quietly or secretly, exercising no liturgical role or pastoral office, having certain teaching positions in Catholic schools closed to him.[29]

One important and recent modification in this legislative scheme relates to the diaconate. The Second Vatican Council, in restoring the ancient office of the permanent diaconate, stated that the order could be conferred upon mature married men.[30] Subsequent enabling legislation made possible the ordination of married men to a major order in the Latin Church for the first time in many centuries. However, it also provided that those who

[24] C. 132, par. 3.
[25] C. 133, par. 1.
[26] C. 133, pars. 3 & 4, cf. Cc. 2176ss, 2358, par. 1.
[27] Cc. 1072, 2388.par.1, 985; *Lex Sacri Caelibatus*, S. Penit., 18 April 1936, A.A.S., 28 (1936) 242.
[28] Cc. 211ss, The m.p. *De Episcoporum Muneribus*, IX, 1, gives bishops the authority to dispense subdeacons, 15 June 1966, A.A.S., 58 (1966) 470.
[29] A.A.S., 63 (1971) 303ss.
[30] *The Constitution on the Church*, art. 29.

have received the order of deacon may not afterwards contract marriage.[31]

When and under what circumstances was this legislation on priestly celibacy enacted? A brief historical overview should be helpful here:[32]

(*a*) for the first three centuries no restraints were imposed on the clergy with regard to marriage; up to the end of the fourth century those engaged in the pastoral service of the Church were usually married; not as a concession to weakness, but as the ordinary way of life;

(*b*) the earliest prohibition against the use of marriage by bishops, priests and deacons—at the Spanish Council of Elvira in 306—was in a distinctly rigoristic context; there was a tendency to sacralize ministerial offices; some extreme groups disparaged married life; cultic purity was a clearly stated motive for sexual abstinence; the Council of Nicaea (325) refused to make the rule of Elvira a general requirement;

(*c*) the Eastern tradition developed between the early fourth and late seventh centuries to be finally confirmed in the Council of Trullo (691): deacons and priests may be married before their ordination, not afterwards, and bishops are not to be married;

(*d*) the Western Church continued to develop towards a celibate discipline, largely encouraged by decretals of popes (Siricius, Innocent, Leo) accepted and reinforced in local councils (Rome, Toledo, Carthage, Turin, Orange, Tours) in the late fourth and fifth centuries; subdeacons were now included in the prohibition because of their service at the altar; the discipline was not uniform and apparently enforced unevenly;

(*e*) in the sixth and seventh centuries the invasions from the north caused the Empire to collapse and the popes (e.g., Gregory, Pelagius) sought in vain to maintain or restore clerical discipline; clerical marriage was prevalent;

(*f*) the eighth and ninth centuries witnessed the growth of monasticism, the influence of the monk-missionaries and the reform councils of the Carolingians—all gave testimony to the

---

[31] *Sacrum Diaconatus Ordinem*, III, 18 June 1967; A.A.S., 59 (1967) 701.

[32] This survey is based in part on John E. Lynch, "Marriage and Celibacy of the Clergy, The Discipline of the Western Church: An Historico-Canonical Synopsis", *The Jurist*, 32 (1972), pp. 14–38.

ideal of clerical continence and the partially successful attempts to realize that ideal;

(g) in the tenth and eleventh centuries the dignity and sacredness of the priestly office were often lost to the greed and control of the feudal lords; clerical marriage and concubinage were widespread despite determined voices raised in protest and condemnation;

(h) the long struggle, rooted in monasticism, known as the Gregorian Reform (ca. 1050–1150) succeeded gradually in establishing at least a norm of clerical celibacy; by means of local councils, visitations and stern letters, Leo IX and the following popes took strong action against violators; polemical writings argued both sides of the issue and the very practical problems of supporting a priest's family, the inheritance of church property and the purchase of offices for the children of bishops, etc., figured large in the policies pursued; in many areas the discipline proved unenforceable;

(i) the most radical single piece of legislation in this long history was that enacted by the Second Lateran Council in 1139 (and reiterated at Lateran IV in 1215), which declared the marriages of clerics to be null and void—no marriages at all; previously they were simply considered to be illicit, illegal;

(j) John Gratian's classic canonical collection (*Concordantia Discordantium Canonum*) of 1140 pulled together many conflicting texts, but reinforced the discipline of the Gregorian Reform;

(k) the frequently repeated admonitions and censures of the popes and local councils in the twelfth and thirteenth centuries attest to the fact that clerical celibacy was far from firmly established; the extent of the nonconformity is very difficult to estimate;

(l) certainly concubinage continued to be a serious problem up to and through the Reformation and Counter-Reform periods; the abuse was apparently widespread at times, but it probably did not predominate in most areas: the wisdom and prudence of the legislation on celibacy continued to be discussed in connection with the major reform councils: Vienne (1311–12), Constance (1414–18), Florence (1431–45), Lateran V (1512–17) and Trent (1545–63).

The foregoing hasty historical sketch recalls to mind the vicissitudes of the policy of priestly celibacy. It would be simplistic to describe it as the story of the upper clergy's efforts to keep the lower clergy chaste and dutiful, yet often it appears that the experiences and insights of the priests themselves were not seriously considered.

The present law is an accumulation of pastoral admonitions, administrative regulations and punitive censures which have been gathered from centuries of attempts to keep the Western Catholic clergy unmarried and continent. The law is harsh, but for the most part effective.

III. A RECOMMENDED COURSE OF ACTION

Celibacy is not a dead issue; it has never been completely at rest in the Church. Even in the aftermath of an extensive debate, a synodal decision and a papal confirmation, the problem remains. It lingers partly because the positive values of a married clergy working alongside a celibate clergy were not carefully considered in the synod's discussions—the personal, pastoral and ecumenical advantages were not explored. But mainly the question of optional celibacy remains because the priests have not changed their minds. They are simply not persuaded that the Gospel is more effectively proclaimed, the people better served and their own lives more truly Christlike because of a universal regulation against marriage.

The solution to the nagging problem lies in change; there is need for a calm and gradual, planned and prayerful transition to a discipline which permits married priests and still fosters the charism of celibacy. It must be kept in mind that the purpose of such a change is to provide the Church with the service of priests who are spiritual and religious leaders of outstanding human qualities.

The following recommendations are offered as guidelines for measured change:[33]

[33] These recommendations are substantially those which emanated from a symposium on "The Future Discipline of Priestly Celibacy", sponsored by the Canon Law Society of America, and held in New York in August 1971.

(a) Principles for a Period of Transition

The first need is to plan for a period of gradual transition, re-flection and experience. Only thorough preparation and decisive leadership will assure the Church of the necessary assimilation process. This process should be directed towards a greater flexi-bility of Christian ministries as well as towards the positive accep-tance of married men in the order of priests.

The whole Church must assess the experience of a limited number of married men in the ministry. During this period of controlled implementation decisions can be made reasonably for the good of these men and for the welfare of the Church and the local churches.

Even a limited introduction of married men into the order of priests will entail a wider sharing of responsibility in the hier-archy of bishops, priests and deacons and within the laity. All should be open to the movement of the Spirit in the development of new institutions, areas of responsibility and styles of life for priests who have received the sacrament of marriage as well as for priests whose lives bear the witness of celibacy for the sake of the King-dom.

The restoration of the married diaconate offers a paradigm of flexibility and adaptability. During the period of transition and initial experience, flexibility should not be hampered by the promulgation of specific rules for universal implementation. This flexibility will demand great discretion and responsibility throughout the Church, but these in turn will benefit both the development of married ministry and the preservation and pro-motion of celibate ministry as a genuine option.

(b) Competence of the Local Church

The needs of the Christian people differ widely throughout the world, in the older churches and the young churches, where there are many priests and where there are few, among nations of diverse cultures. The primary responsibility for directing the life and ministry of priests, both celibate and married, should reside in the local church, but in full consultation with the other local churches of the ecclesiastical province. The very plurality of ministries in response to diverse conditions demands respect for the principle of subsidiarity in decision-making.

The decision to admit a married man to the priesthood should be made for the spiritual good of the community and faithful he will serve, that is, for the local church. The local bishop should have the principal role in the concrete and individual decision within the church over which he presides. But his decision may not be made arbitrarily or without serious consideration of the good of the whole Church and the other churches. He should feel bound to follow a procedure of prudent and extensive consultation with his presbyteral senate, the diocesan pastoral council, and other members of the laity and the ordained ministry. Because of common needs and problems, he should consult also with the bishops of the ecclesiastical province.

The episcopal conference should have the authority to exercise surveillance in this matter. The local bishop should, therefore, report his decision to the conference, but unless his decision works positive harm to the Church, he should be presumed to have acted for the spiritual good of the faithful. The episcopal conference should submit, during the period of transition, a yearly report to Rome for the purpose of world-wide information and co-ordination.

(c) Preparation of the Church

In this time of transition the entire Church must be prepared for the acceptance of the ministry of married priests. This holds even for regions which do not seem ready for such a development, in view of the influence of modern communications and in preparation for the future. Both ordained ministers and laity should be helped to appreciate the diversity of gifts within the Church. The faithful should see in the married priest and his wife an example of marriage in Christ, as they see in the celibate priest the sign of a different Christian gift and witness. They should be ready to give special assistance and support to celibate priests.

Local bishops should initiate a positive catechesis through conferences, lectures, writings and programmes of information. The purpose of these efforts is to acquaint the people with a genuinely Christian understanding of the priestly ministry and its actual or possible diversification among married and unmarried men. In this educational process it is important to consult with the Orthodox and with Protestants, in order to benefit from their Christian experience of a married ministry.

Accompanying such catechesis should be programmes of theological and pastoral research to examine the Christian significance of ministry in the service of the Lord and his people, the relation of ministry to the diverse gifts of celibacy and marriage, and the dimensions of the problem of the clerical state.

(d) Canonical Norms

The initial introduction of married priests, or even a more profound study of the question in the Church's life, will necessarily entail an investigation of the canonical discipline affecting ordained ministers.

The good of individual ministers and the good of the Church call for openness to different ministries according to the needs and expectations of the Catholic people. The local bishop must be free to adjust canonical norms regarding offices and responsibilities to new situations. The married status of the priest and the needs of his wife and family must be considered; the transfer of the priest from one local church to another must be simplified.

The canon law concerning the preparation of priests should be accommodated to provide for the pastoral and theological training of married priests, depending on their background, the local or regional situation, the needs of the ministry in general or of a particular ministerial role.

Provision for financial support of married priests and their families is a prerequisite, but will vary according to the conditions of a full-time or part-time ministry.

In both law and fact the married priest must have equal status with celibate priests within the presbyterium. This applies particularly to his participation in the decision-making process of the local church and to his part in the determination of his own ministry. At the same time it is important that the celibate priest not be placed at a disadvantage in such matters as ministry and support.

Bishops and other ministers should feel obliged to show, on a personal and individual basis, deep concern for the growth in faith and in the life of prayer by all priests and deacons, both married and unmarried.

Certain canonical obstacles related to the ministry and celibacy should be suppressed, e.g., (1) the diriment matrimonial impediment of sacred orders, (ii) the excommunication of a cleric who attempts civil marriage, and (iii) the prohibition of remarriage to permanent deacons. The acceptance of the resignation of an ordained minister, priest or deacon, from the active exercise of the ministry should be with the authority of the local church.

PART II
DOCUMENTATION

Richard A. Schoenherr

Holy Power? Holy Authority? and Holy Celibacy?

THE AIM of this article is to analyse a number of sociological issues regarding power, authority and celibacy in a changing church order. As part of the analysis I shall report some of the data we collected for the national study of the Catholic priesthood in the United States commissioned by the National Conference of U.S. Bishops.[1]

Much of the concern over the priesthood has received popular notice because of the sometimes thoughtful and sometimes clamorous discussions about celibacy. The discipline of priestly celibacy is a difficult question in its own right. It is further complicated, however, because it has become one of the tightest knots in the tangled authority conflict currently facing the Church. We shall examine the celibacy issue in the context of the closely related topics of ecclesiastical power and authority.

The Catholic Church, like all giant formal organizations, is a complex social system. This means in effect that the maintenance and adjustment of the whole Church are dependent upon the equilibrium of a network of somewhat autonomous and interdependent parts. I have in mind here analytically distinct system parts rather than the more easily identifiable geographic subdivisions such as national churches, provinces and dioceses.

[1] The full 486-page report, titled *American Priests*, was prepared at the National Opinion Research Center of the University of Chicago by Andrew M. Greeley and Richard A. Schoenherr, principal and co-principal investigators; it has been scheduled for publication in book-form by the United States Catholic Conference in 1972.

At a higher level of abstraction we may consider the three major system parts of the Church as the administrative, operational and membership subsystems. Pope and bishops, as the administrative subsystem, bear the responsibility of controlling and co-ordinating the myriad activities of the Church. Priests and religious have the duty, as the operational subsystem, of carrying out the actual operations involved in caring for the pastoral and spiritual needs of the people. The Catholic faithful, who comprise the membership subsystem, assume the task of integrating Christian beliefs and values into their personal lives and social patterns.

From a social system viewpoint, each of the three subsystems of the Church has a vitally important but essentially different function to perform. The members of each group possess their own resources and talents which they must maintain and draw upon to achieve their goals. They have different needs and problems, some of which are so unique as to be unintelligible to others who belong to a different subsystem. It is necessary for an organization's parts to maintain a set of structural boundaries to protect their autonomy and ensure their own internal balance. The protection of subsystem boundaries permits members to use their resources for the best advantage of the whole system only if the system parts maintain a sufficient level of interdependence. The interdependence of subsystems is too often taken for granted, when in reality it is very problematic. In commenting on the importance of reciprocity and autonomy in complex organizations, Alvin Gouldner, a well-known American sociologist, writes:

... a basic source of organizational tension may derive, on the one hand, from the tendency of the parts to resist encroachment of their functional autonomy and, on the other, from contrary tendencies of the organization's controlling centre to limit or reduce the functional autonomy of the parts.[2]

Tension among the parts is one of the facts of organizational life. Just to be able to perform the tasks for which they are re-

[2] Alvin W. Gouldner, "Organizational Analysis", in *Sociology Today*, Robert K. Merton, Leonard Broom and Leonard S. Cattrell, Jr. (eds.) (New York, 1965), p. 420.

sponsible, Pope, bishops, priests and people must sometimes jealously husband their resources, push their point of view, engage in confrontation, and generally protect themselves against encroachment from other members of the Church who belong to a different subsystem. This type of organizational behaviour is not necessarily malicious or unchristian because it involves conflict. It is absolutely essential so that the autonomous system parts can both achieve their goals and maintain their interdependence. Conflict is a necessary process even in a sacred social system.

Conflict should be openly faced by the members of an organization rather than repressed, because without honest confrontation the interdependence of system parts can be weakened and even destroyed. It is a paradox that an organization is held together by its cleavages and boundary maintenance mechanisms.

The celibacy issue has become a source of conflict between the administrative and operational subsystems of the Church. Predictably, there is more effort on the part of the "formal hierarchy of authority" to repress this conflict than to resolve it head on. A resolution of the conflict would require formal bargaining procedures which would directly challenge the monocratic authority structure of the present-day Church. It appears that modification in the present regulations prohibiting marriage for priests is stymied because of the lack of adequate conflict resolution mechanisms. Hence, the celibacy problem, as we shall see, is part of a much deeper and more pervasive conflict over power and authority.

Social systems manage to survive and continue to work as long as the major system parts somehow remain interdependent in spite of their individual autonomy. Authority is a crucial social mechanism that helps to unify the parts of a complex organization. The Church cannot get along without adequate authority relationships, just as no other human organization can do so. At the base of the ecclesiastical authority crisis is an obsolete and woefully inadequate authority structure, one that is grounded on a tottering theoretical notion of what power and authority are. Before presenting the findings from the study of American bishops and priests that are pertinent to an understanding of the Church's current power struggle and celibacy debate, it is neces-

sary to stake out some common ground on which to base a discussion of power and authority.

Authority affects everyone because it has to do with how power
is to be used. Power means the capacity to accomplish one's goals
in spite of opposition from others. It can take many forms ranging
from brute strength to gentle persuasion. Power in the abstract is
a neutral commodity. The use of power is judged as good or
evil depending on the intentions and objective goals of the user.

Since power is a pervasive part of human life and human organizations, its use must be carefully channelled and socially
controlled. Authority is the social relationship that stabilizes the
use of power so that the members of a social system can enjoy a
proper distribution of scarce resources. Authority civilizes the use
of power. Christian authority, we would hope, baptizes the use of
power.

The first point to emphasize about authority, then, is that it
deals with the use of power. Secondly, I would emphasize the
fact that it is a social relationship between superior and subordinates. No one ever *possesses* authority all by himself. Authority is
usually defined erroneously in theological terms as a possession
of the superior given to him by God. Since we are concerned
with ecclesiastical authority it is especially necessary to call attention to the importance of viewing authority always as a relationship rather than a possession.

Max Weber, a classical writer in sociology, emphasizes the re-
lational aspects when he defines authority as "the probability that
certain commands from a given source will be obeyed by a given
group of persons". The basic criterion of authority is a "certain
minimum of voluntary submission" and the criterion of maxi-
mum authority would be "unquestioning obedience". Hence, in
the final analysis, if there is no willing obedience, no authority
relationship exists.

Undermining and eventually destroying the authority relationship is the preserve of the process that establishes and maintains
the legitimate use of power. If in the collective judgment of the
followers the leader ceases to provide satisfactory services, the
legitimization of his power may be gradually rescinded and the
authority relationship destroyed. First a growing number of followers disapproves of the leader's commands and so begins to dis-

obey them. After a time collective disapproval is generated. Simultaneously the norms and sanctions that were once invoked to punish deviants are gradually relaxed and eventually removed. Wilful disobedience becomes the rule rather than the exception. When compliance with the majority of the leader's commands becomes too costly for the group, his authority may be over-thrown, or merely ignored if the needed resources can be gotten from someone else.

Several conclusions from the sociological theory of authority should be underlined:

1. Superiors cannot establish their own authority; it is given to them by their subordinates. As leaders they can maintain the strength of the authority position by continuing to provide those services that win the collective approval of the followers.

2. When positions of authority remain unchanged, but the in-cumbents' commands are no longer obeyed, the superiors have *powerless* authority. This is true because a high probability of obedience no longer exists.

3. The distribution of power in an organization is constantly fluctuating since its members and environment are always chang-ing. The patterns of authority, therefore, must also be subject to change. It is critical for the success of an organization that those members who have the needed resources also have the use of their powers legitimated by the total collectivity. Outmoded positions of authority, whose incumbents no longer possess the power and resources to warrant the extent of their authority, create weak-ness and strain in the organization. If many managerial positions become positions of powerless authority, the members suffer be-cause the organization lacks the vital direction and control neces-sary to achieve its goals.

4. A healthy and, we might add in this context, a holy orga-nization is one in which there is the right balance of centralized and decentralized authority, one in which the distribution of authority is effectively based on the *de facto* distribution of power. Hence the administrative subsystem of the Church should not have a monopoly on the use of authority, for the simple reason that it does not contain all the resources and responsibilities of the ecclesiastical organization. The operational subsystem must be given the authority necessary to exploit its resources to their best

advantage and so make its proper contribution to the achievement of the common good of the total Church. The same must be said of the membership subsystem and the need to recognize the authority of the laity in fulfilling their responsibilities.

This theoretical background provides an appropriate context in which to discuss the meaning of the sociological data gathered from a random sample of 5,155 diocesan and religious priests and 165 bishops in the United States. (Although much of the analysis would apply to the relationships existing between the laity and the other two major system parts of the Church, unfortunately the data to be presented are limited almost exclusively to information about bishops and priests. Accordingly, I can consider the lay membership only tangentially in the following discussion.) I shall begin with an analysis of the data delineating the authority conflict between the administrators and the operational personnel of the Church.

It is evident from the responses to several items on our questionnaire that ecclesiastical authority is being eroded by both sides of the authority relationship, by those in the superordinate as well as by those in the subordinate positions. In examining our tables and figures we discovered that the priests, for their part, very frequently take stands on moral issues that are diametrically opposed to the official positions held by the Pope and bishops. For example, we find that with regard to birth control, only two-fifths of the priests of all ages and slightly more than one-fifth of those forty-five and younger agree with the magisterium's official position that "the faithful are bound to avoid all methods of artificial contraception". The age-bracket "forty-five and younger" includes exactly half of the total number of priests in the United States. A comparison of the figures in the submitted report shows an astounding sixty-one percentage points difference—eighty-three per cent vs. twenty-two per cent—between the bishops and the younger half of the clergy in the proportion endorsing the "official" attitude towards birth control.

A similar picture unfolded when the priests were asked their opinions concerning divorce and remarriage. Again, only two-fifths of all priests and slightly less than one-fifth of the younger half of the clergy said that they adhere to the official position that "divorce with the freedom to remarry in the case of a marriage *ratum et consummatum* can never be permitted by the Church". A full four-fifths of the bishops, on the other hand, reported agreement with the official stand on both birth control and divorce.

A continuing deterioration of clerical support for the official birth control position is clearly evident in a related number of findings. The data discussed above reflect attitudes and confessional procedures since the appearance of the encyclical *Humanae Vitae*. The respondents were also questioned about what their attitude and procedure had been before *Humanae Vitae*. A comparison of the two sets of responses showed that twenty-seven per cent of the priests are now more "liberal" in their attitudes and twenty-nine per cent are more lenient in handling birth-control problems in the confessional since the encyclical than they remembered being before it was promulgated. Only three or four per cent took more "conservative" positions after *Humanae Vitae* while the vast majority—sixty-six and seventy per cent—did not change at all. If the encyclical was meant to reinforce endorsement of the official position on birth control, it turned out to be counter-productive in the balance.

The apparent failure of the encyclical to stem the dissent and disobedience among priests can easily be linked with the pervasive feeling that *Humanae Vitae* was not a legitimate exercise of papal authority. When asked their opinion on the matter, only a minority of the priests were willing to accept the encyclical as a competent and appropriate use of the teaching authority of the papacy.

Our questionnaire was designed to enable us to examine the authority relationships between the administrative and operational subsystems as they are reflected in the distribution of influence in the local diocesan church. From the responses to a pertinent set of items we discovered that there is hardly any disagreement among bishops and priests about the actual distribution of authority or influence in a diocese. In every age category the vast majority—from ninety-five to ninety-nine per cent—sees the bishop as having all the authority and influence in "determining policies and actions in the dioceses". Chancery officials are considered to be somewhat influential, but no one else has much influence according to the priests' perceptions of the situation. The bishops, however, are somewhat more likely than priests to perceive that others also possess influence.

When asked about who *ought* to have influence in determining policies and actions in the diocese, once again large majorities —from eighty-five to ninety-six per cent—of both priests and bishops favoured a strong position of authority for the bishop. But priests were more likely than bishops—sixty-three per cent vs. fifty-three per cent—to want to see a great deal of influence in the hands of the priests' senate. In the minds of priests of all ages, the priests' senate was the second most popular locus of influence after the bishop, but in the judgment of the bishops the chancery should retain the second place.

The amount of influence that ought to accrue to the priests' senate emerges as the critical issue. Interestingly enough, approximately half of the bishops were willing to say the senate *should* have considerable influence; but that is exactly the same proportion of bishops who believed that the priests' senate *already had* a great deal of influence. The differences in the perceptions and judgments of the bishops and priests are extremely telling, for only one-fifth of the priests think their senates *have* a great deal of influence at the present time whereas three-fifths think that they *should* have a great deal of influence. There is, then, a strong desire among priest-members of the operational subsystem to increase the authority of the priests' senate, but apparently no sentiment among bishops for increasing the level of recognized power for the priests' senate. In other words, the organizational change to redistribute influence and authority that the priests are most likely to want is the one the bishops are least likely to support.

Along with differences in opinion about decision-making power in dioceses there is also sharp disagreement about what more general reforms would help the Church. For example, approximately three-quarters of the priests are in favour of the election of a pope by the synod of bishops and the election of bishops by the priests of the diocese. However, comparable figures for the bishops on these two reforms show only minority support for such institutional changes. Both changes would be important steps in the direction of loosening the rigid control of authority that rests in the hands of the administrative subsystem. It is also worth noting that while two-fifths of the bishops favour the election of a pope by bishops, only one-fourth of them endorse the election of bishops by their priests.

A definite pattern emerges from these data. Collective disregard of authoritative commands is fairly widespread, especially among the younger half of the clergy in the United States. And, judging from the amount of internal dissent against official teachings and proscriptions, there exists a large potential for further disobedience in practice. A conflict over the legitimate use of power is evident: the bishops see no particular need for change in authority relations, the priests display strong sympathy for change, and the younger priests are the ones most likely to endorse change. Our data provide ample documentation that those charged with the task of co-ordination and control of the Church are convinced that their responsibility is strenuously to resist any encroachment on their monopoly of authority by the priest-members of the operational subsystems.

What general conclusions can we draw from this partial sketch of the priesthood and the Church in the United States? It seems evident to me that authority relationships, which are vital for the integration and co-ordination of the Church's efforts, are being seriously undermined. Ecclesiastical authority is being critically weakened by both sides of the relationship, not just by priests but by bishops and Pope as well.

Priests, for their part, are taking stands on moral issues that are in clear opposition to established authority. They are exercising initiative in proscribed liturgical areas and are administering sacraments in a manner forbidden by the centralized rules and regulations of the Church. Substantial numbers of them feel, on the basis of their own pastoral skill and competence, that they ought to have the authority to use their own judgment in these ways. Many priests think that authority should be redistributed, and are especially convinced that the autonomous use of their own pastoral expertise ought to be legitimated by establishing the priests' senate as a locus of authority in the Church. The large proportion of priests acting in keeping with these convictions reflects a growing disapproval of the way leadership is being exercised by those in the top administrative positions. Their collective disobedience, in effect, is destroying authority relationships, because without willing obedience authority does not exist.

Bishops, on the other hand, display very little enthusiasm about changing the authority pattern of the local, the national or the international Church. They consider themselves to have full authority and want little or no change in the authority arrangements. This means that the bishops staunchly support the centralized bureaucratic authority patterns of the Church, and in supporting them they are contributing to the erosion of authority itself. They are, in effect, allowing the position of bishop to become one of *powerless* authority.

If these conflicts remain unresolved, authority relationships throughout the Church will simply collapse. Those entrusted with the control and co-ordination of the Church as a social system will possess powerless authority as more and more directives are ignored and collective sanctions become ineffective. If authority is not redistributed so that the use of power is legitimated at a level more in keeping with where the actual resources lie, in keeping with principles of collegiality rather than principles of bureaucracy, the whole Church and all its members will suffer accordingly.

By seeing the celibacy issue in its proper perspective, as bound up with the authority crisis, we can better understand why it is raising such a hue and cry. The redefinition and redistribution of authority is a slow process, and gradualism of reform can be tolerable for highly committed members of the Church. But, from the individual priest's point of view, there cannot be a gradual solution to the celibacy question. If an individual priest wants to marry, regardless of his degree of commitment to the Church and ministry, he is forced to resign from the public exercise of his office. Alarming numbers of priests in the United States are resolving the problem in this way.

In an earlier study of the priesthood, Joseph Fichter, s.j., discovered that during the two and one-half decades prior to the Second Council of the Vatican, the annual voluntary resignation rate for diocesan priests in the United States did not rise much above one-tenth of one per cent.[3] Then, in the nineteen-sixties,

[3] *America's Forgotten Priests* (New York). The annual rate was computed from the average of the cumulative percentages presented by Fichter

the number of priests giving up their public affiliation with the priesthood—applying for dispensations or not—began to rise sharply. According to our own highly accurate data and others collected by the Gallup organization, the annual rate climbed from one-half of one per cent in 1966 to a current rate of nearly four per cent per annum in 1972.[4] We can conclude from the annual rates that the Roman Catholic Church in the United States has suffered the cumulative loss of over one-eighth of its clergy through resignations in less than seven years.

In absolute figures, the number of American priests who left the public ministry between the beginning of 1966 and 1972 stood at 8,000 give or take a few hundred. By the end of the current year the total will be close to 10,000. To put the voluntary departure problem in an historical perspective, in the last seven years the climbing rate of resignations has increased thirty- and perhaps fortyfold over the preceding twenty-five years. These data indicate a problem for the Church and the priesthood of crisis proportions.

Whatever might have been the cause of the almost unnoticeable resignation rates of the recent past, the enormous increase in voluntary withdrawals that we are currently witnessing is due in great part to the restriction on marriage for priests. When we asked the active priests and a sample of priests who had already resigned what they thought was the first or second most important reason why priests leave the ministry, the desire to marry was the most frequently cited cause.

The explanation resulting from a further very detailed analysis of the data may be summarized as follows: if marriage is perceived as a desirable life-style; if loneliness produces personal problems that outweigh the rewards provided by the present situation; if one's values and attitudes about the priesthood and

---

as grouped data for the ordination classes of 1943 to 1966. These are the only data for the United States we know of covering this period. They were obtained by asking the respondents in a mailed survey, "How many priests were there in your ordination class?" and "As far as you know, how many of these have left the priesthood?"

[4] The data for 1966–69 were collected by the National Opinion Research Center from official resignation records provided by diocesan chanceries and provincial headquarters of religious communities, and were verified in several ways to make them as accurate as possible.

marriage are changing by becoming more open; and if leaving the diocese or religious congregation is made easier by being relatively young: a priest is likely to decide to resign and take up some other occupation.

These findings raise a question of considerable importance for the future discipline of priestly celibacy: why has the restriction on marriage suddenly become so salient a part of the commitment decision of Catholic priests? The answer to that question, I believe, can be found by examining the essential values pertaining to the Christian priesthood as they are viewed by today's priest.

It appears that belief in the personal value of celibacy is diminishing among Catholic clergymen. Although three-fourths of the priests in the United States feel that celibacy is an advantage for doing their work better, only a little over half describe it as an advantage for developing their love for God, for relating more fully to the other people, and for aiding personal growth and development. Majority support among the younger half of the priests can be found only for the statement that celibacy is an asset for doing their work better, and not for the other three modes of growth and development.

A number of items in the questionnaire were designed to tap the priest's values regarding celibacy as reflected in the more general context of his attitudes towards human sexuality. A careful examination of the data shows that whereas the majority of bishops and older priests endorse those "traditional" values that would support the restriction on marriage, only a minority of the younger priests agree with such statements. On the other hand, the majority of younger priests agree with the "modern" statements that reflect values supporting marriage as an option for Catholic priests, whereas only a minority of bishops and older priests are willing to accept these statements.

Therefore it is not surprising to discover that well over half of all priests and over three-fourths of the younger ones agree that celibacy should be made optional, whereas one-tenth of the bishops are in favour of dropping the restriction on marriage. Furthermore, for all but the bishops and the oldest category of priests, the overwhelming majority of the clergy *expect* a change in the law of celibacy; and of those who expect change, three-quarters think it will come within the next ten years.

These data reveal that many priests do not believe strongly in the value of the type of sacrifice they are making. A different set of values and attitudes is creating a strain towards a new state of consistency that will balance values and action. This strain is especially strong among the young priests, whose beliefs in the religious advantages of celibacy are the weakest and whose problems with loneliness are the greatest. Among those for whom celibacy is not highly valued the restriction on marriage is perceived as too great or too meaningless a prerequisite for the priesthood. Hence a decision to leave the ministry is made in order to restore consistency and balance to one's life.

It also appears that the traditionally strong negative sanctions from the laity against those who leave the ministry and marry have been considerably relaxed recently. On the basis of a study conducted for the National Federation of Priests Councils and another study conducted by the Office of Planning and Research in the Archdiocese of Detroit, we know that a majority of the United States Catholic laity of all age groups are now in favour of "allowing Catholic priests to marry and continue to function as priests" and would even "welcome a married priest to their own parish". This increasing collective acceptance of the possibility of a married clergy no doubt facilitates the decision to leave the ministry in order to marry. Since almost three-tenths of American priests forty-five years of age and younger reported in 1970 that they would probably or certainly marry if celibacy for priests became optional, resignations from the public ministry may be expected to continue at the current high rates for some time to come.

The losses sustained by the Church in terms of numbers are indeed great, but the loss in terms of quality may prove to be an equally important consideration. It is possible to assess "quality" in terms of personal maturity, a high level of advanced education, an openness to improving values and attitudes regarding Church and priesthood, and, in an important sense, simple youthfulness. In our national study of American priests we discovered that among those who left or are planning to leave there are higher proportions of more mature, better educated, more open and younger men than among those who were remaining in the active ministry. If these dimensions reflect desirable qualities in the priest, the qualitative loss is at least as alarming as the rising numbers.

The facts of the situation are clearly evident from the data. The American hierarchy and the older priests are strongly opposed to changing the Church's discipline regarding sacerdotal celibacy. However, the overwhelming majority of all other priests and well over half of the laity are in favour of permitting men in sacred orders to marry if they wish.

We must conclude that a serious conflict situation over the future discipline of celibacy exists within the Church. It is one that will not be resolved easily because the differences are rooted in quite different values about the nature of celibacy and its connection with the priesthood. The conflict between the hierarchy and the younger members of the priesthood over the celibacy issue is complicated by the fact that it is part of a more general authority conflict between the members of these same two subsystems.

How does the celibacy controversy fit into the authority conflict? From a management point of view, it is in the best interests of the administrative subsystem of the Church, namely, the Pope and the bishops, to want to maintain the discipline of celibacy because a celibate clergy facilitates co-ordination and control. As a latent function, which is to say regardless of whether this consequence is intended or recognized, the restriction on marriage for priests creates a well-disciplined and easily controlled group of religious professionals who are ready to carry out Church responsibilities without being restricted by family duties. Many priests, on the other hand, feel that the option of marriage would be more in keeping with their values as well as the needs of the ministry. So, from the viewpoint of the priests who comprise the operational subsystem, enforced celibacy may be considered an encroachment on the autonomy and flexibility needed in their ministry and their personal lives.

The celibacy issue may be interpreted as a power conflict, then, in that the Pope and bishops do not want to abolish mandatory celibacy because it would mean the loss of the power to control and co-ordinate their religious personnel. Further, if the bishops succumbed to the pressure of their priests and insisted in Rome on optional celibacy, they would thereby recognize the powerful influence of their priests. The bishops would be recognizing the power and ability of their priests to choose what is right for themselves and their pastoral ministry. If a pope, in turn, yielded to the insistence of a national hierarchy and decided to allow the option to marry for priests, he would be admitting that he should not make such decisions on his own judgment.

In both instances, a weakening of the tightly centralized decision-making authority of the Church administration would result. The Pope would be relinquishing authority to the bishops and the bishops would be relinquishing authority to the priests. In a highly bureaucratized organization such a loss of centralized control is very undesirable from a management viewpoint.

On the other side of the conflict, priests strongly support changes that will widen the options of their ministry, but they find they have no influence to change the law that imposes celibacy. They base their convictions on their own personal and pastoral considerations. Since they are indeed the acting pastoral ministers of the Church, they see the change as necessary from the operational viewpoint. The open debate about celibacy has all the makings of a critical power conflict at various levels in the Church. Power conflicts that are rooted in value differences tend to be much more serious, pervasive and long-lasting than power struggles among those who share the same set of values.

From a purely sociological perspective, it is my conviction that a married clergy in the Latin rite is inevitable. The change in values and attitudes evident in the data presented here represents a long and slow process and one that is very difficult to reverse. The amount of time it takes to bring about change is contingent upon the amount of success that priests and bishops have in redefining and redistributing authority in the Church.

Several problems directly related to the authority conflict must be handled simultaneously as the celibacy issue is resolved. The Roman Curia and the national hierarchies will have to come to terms on the proper balance between centralized and decentralized authority. Bishops, priests and laity in the national churches will likewise have to discover and admit where the power and resources exist and learn how to legitimate the use of that power in the eyes of all the members of the Church. The members of both the administrative and the operational subsystems must become more comfortable in acknowledging and respecting their own power and more efficient in learning how to mobilize it.

The celibacy issue, then, will be settled as bishops vis-à-vis the Roman Curia and priests vis-à-vis the national hierarchies learn how to convert their possible power into realized power. According to Dennis Wrong, in a masterful essay on social power, social groups can convert possible power into realized power only by the "achievement of solidarity, common goals, social organization and leadership".[5] Many national hierarchies as a group are well on their way to achieving all four conditions; priests, however, have a long way to go before they achieve realized power. If priests as a group are able to speed up the process of acquiring solidarity, setting some common goals, establishing social organization and acquiring leadership, the future discipline of celibacy may well be decided within the ten years' time projected by many respondents in our study.

No one denies that there will be many difficulties and mistakes attending the transition from a celibate to a married clergy. These are the inevitable pains accompanying change that have been aptly labelled "the liabilities of newness". The Church is a human organization and so will change in the manner of all organizations, that is, with slow incremental steps. The change must take place in terms of more "knowns" than "unknowns". And we find that the first small steps have already been taken with the ordination of married deacons. The next hesitant step will no doubt be the ordaining of already married men to the full ranks of the priesthood. This is so fearful, if inevitable, a next step that last fall the synod fathers refused to take it collectively. They preferred instead to let the matter rest with the Pope —an ominous reinforcement of the rigid centralization of authority.

It would be most unfortunate to try to suppress the conflict and disagreements that are bound to arise during the time of transition; for to do so would undoubtedly bury some valuable insights and cause the members of the conflicting groups to with-

[5] Dennis H. Wrong, "Some Problems in Defining Social Power", *American Journal of Sociology*, 73 (1968), p. 680.

draw and eventually ignore one another. There are ways to balance the liabilities of newness with the assets of experience. The Roman Church, for example, can learn from other Christian churches and the Catholic clergy can accept the counsel of other ministers. A married clergy faces a somewhat different set of problems from those affecting a celibate clergy, but it is completely useless to speculate on theoretical grounds whether one set is more severe than the other. This is once again an empirical question. But the many practical details surrounding the complex problems of power, authority and celibacy can never be solved without honest conflict and struggle. And solutions may be reached without the help of a spirit of love, trust and loyalty unless we soon attend to the baptism of even so ugly and human a thing as our power struggles.

Sebastian Kappen

Priestly Celibacy in India

TO WRITE an objective report on the question of celibacy in India is wellnigh impossible. For in this matter truth tends to hide itself in the sphere either of the strictly personal or of the collective subconscious. It seldom emerges to the realm of free and open discussion. And this for the following reasons: First, discussion in public of anything connected with sex is still taboo in Indian society. Second, there is an all-pervasive, repressive fear: fear on the part of the individual priest that any criticism of the law of celibacy would be interpreted by others as motivated by the desire to marry, and fear on the part of the hierarchy that any slackening of the present law may eventually undermine traditional structures.

I. The Pre-Synod Survey

However the veil of fear and secrecy lifted partly at the time of the survey conducted by the Clergy Commission of the Catholic Bishops Conference of India (CBCI) in preparation for the recent synod. Still only a few popular publications dared to invite discussion on the topic.[1] The survey itself belied all expectations. It provided but scanty information and no statistical data. Its main conclusion ran: "The overwhelming majority agrees that

---

[1] For a popular discussion of the topic see letters to the Editor in *The New Leader* (Madras), Vol. 62 (1971), Nos. 26, 28, 35, 47, 48, 49, 50; Vol. 63 (1972), Nos. 1, 5, 8.

even today celibacy remains an ideal of Catholic priesthood."[2] This is interpreted as a clear verdict in favour of the *status quo*. But such an interpretation is unwarranted since recognition of celibacy as *an* ideal need not necessarily mean the rejection of optional celibacy. This ambiguity reflects that of the question itself: "Do you agree that even today celibacy remains an ideal of Catholic priesthood?"[3] Besides, among the questions there was none regarding the concrete problems facing the practice of celibacy.

The vagueness and inadequacy of the questionnaire are matched only by the unsatisfactory manner in which the survey itself was conducted. Not to mention the element of hurry, the procedure adopted in most dioceses was not such as to ensure the free expression of convictions, because either the question-naire was answered in common by assemblies of priests or in-dividual answers were sent to the diocesan curia for scrutiny. In one diocese (Nagpur) the questionnaire was not even shown to all priests. It is probable that the absence of the conditions neces-sary for the sincere expression of views partly explains the poor response from the clergy. Out of 8,000 priests in India only thirty per cent replied. Worst still, only fifteen per cent of the replies came in early enough for scrutiny in view of the final report.[4]

This being the case, the writer found it necessary to supple-ment the official survey with a limited investigation of his own. The method employed consisted in consulting, where possible through intensive interviews, a good number of knowledgeable priests from all over India on the problem of celibacy as experi-enced in their respective regions. The aim was to reduce the margin of error by noting the points of convergence. It is on these that we base our assessments of facts, which are but approxi-mations and admit of regional differences.

II. Symptoms of a Crisis

That the Church in India as a whole is passing through a crisis

[2] *Priestly Ministry*, published by the Clergy Commission of the CBCI (Madura, 1971), p. 26. (The booklet contains, besides the report on the official survey, also the memorandum on Ministerial Priesthood submitted by the CBCI to the synod, 1971).   [3] *Ibid.*   [4] *Ibid.*, p. 5.

is widely recognized.[5] Does this imply that there is also a crisis of priesthood? Many among the senior clergy are still untouched by the changes taking place in and outside the Church. They live in their own world of security provided by traditional ideas and structures. But there are others, among the younger and the more educated priests, who are "doubting and questioning their priestly vocation and mission, and at times the faith on which they are based".[6] According to the official survey they are only a few, which is true enough if we take only those in whom the crisis finds articulate expression. But those who live this crisis are many more than those who think it aloud. Now, any revaluation of priesthood involves also a revaluation of celibacy. For traditionally celibacy was viewed as a prerequisite for priesthood without being invested with any autonomous value. However, it is the reverse process that we find in most priests in crisis. Their central problem was the difficulties experienced in the practice of celibacy. Initially they never questioned the framework of traditional laws. Instead they had recourse to stereotype means like prayer, penance and the avoiding of occasions. Today on the contrary they are questioning the framework itself, thanks mainly to the impact of discussion in the Western Church. Besides, reports about the mass exodus of priests elsewhere served to free them from their inner isolation and give them a sense of solidarity with their colleagues in crisis. Thus the problem of celibacy has become at once radical and socialized.

However, due to various inhibiting factors, the social expression of this crisis is limited. In India there has been no mass exodus of priests. There is however a steady increase in the number of priests who defect, though compared with the total number of the clergy they form only a fraction. We know of only one instance of priests forming an association to contest, among other things, the law of celibacy.[7] The contestants belonged to the archdiocese of Changanacherry and the diocese of Alleppy. Their move met with ruthless disciplinary action and had to be given up. Worth mentioning is also the growing number of seminarians who drop out. Besides, in the opinion of most people we have consulted, quite a few priests seek clandestine sexual satis-

[5] *Ibid.*, p. 7.   [6] *Ibid.*, p. 32.
[7] See report to *The New Leader*, Vol. 62, No. 26 (27 June 1971), p. 7.

faction in one form or another, and their number seems to be on the increase. Some even go to the extent of saying that those who take their celibacy seriously are only a minority.

III. ROOTS OF THE CRISIS

In summarizing the Roman document *De Sacerdotio Minis-teriali* the Clergy Commision says that the present crisis has "its roots in the defective understanding of the meaning and the mission of the Church in the world".[8] While this may be true of some individuals, we should not overlook the fact that the crisis among priests is due largely to their gaining a new understanding of themselves as human persons and as priests, an understanding which, though closer to the Gospel and to our times, is in conflict with the present institutional framework. To grasp this we must reflect on the existential dialogue going on between the priest and the changing secular society in India.

1. *The Challenge of Secularization*

Secularization which is an on-going process in India has created a climate of opposition against Christian institutional activity especially in the field of education. In consequence priests tend to be viewed by the common citizen as unwelcome intruders into their sphere of competence. In places like Kerala where there is a long Christian tradition they have to face also mounting anti-clericalism. Speaking of the priest in north India Archbishop Raymond wrote: "His traditional roles seem to have been taken away from him one by one. Till today he feels unwanted, irrelevant and alienated from the community and an anachronism."[9] Priests are thus forced to withdraw into the sacristy but only to face a further disappointment. For they find that the educated youth have already emigrated, at least mentally, from the Church and that they have to content themselves with doling out "devotions" to the very young or to the very old. All this means not only loss of status and function but also much loneliness and

[8] *The Questionnaire for Priests*, prepared by the Clergy Commission of the CBCI (Madura, 1971).
[9] Quoted by Dr James Kottoor, in his editorial "Hyphenated Priest-hood", *The New Leader*, Vol. 62, No. 14 (4 April 1971), p. 2.

frustration. It is against this background that we must view the problem of celibacy.

2. Towards a New Understanding of Sex

The more direct challenge to celibacy comes from the emergence of new patterns of thinking and acting in sexual matters. The traditional understanding of sex was largely either magical or mythico-religious. In the magical view one thought one could, through sexual activity or its symbolic representation (microcosm), dominate the universal creative force (macrocosm).[10] In the religious view one attributed the fecundity of sex to the direct intervention of gods or of the one God.[11] Even the supreme godhead was conceived as a unity-in-tension between the male and the female (Śiva-Śakti). In either case sex was thought to be controlled by forces outside it. Today, on the contrary, sex is viewed more and more as a human phenomenon with its own immanent meaning and finality. Consequently too, sexual morality is breaking loose from magical and religious taboos. Similarly the traditional emphasis on reproduction is being replaced by a more personalistic approach. This involves also a change in the conception of womanhood. If in the past woman tended to be considered merely as a female, today she is coming into her own as a person. A final point: Though the dominant trend in the past was to affirm the positive value of sex, alongside there existed a minor current of sexual pessimism which in recent centuries became accentuated by contact with the Western puritan tradition. But today the original optimism is being reaffirmed. In sum, a new sex morality is being born out of, or rather alongside, the old.

Faced with these changes the priest becomes a question mark to himself and to the people. He begins to question the spiritual climate of the Christian community which gave birth to and nourished his vocation, a climate charged with sexual pessimism and the sense of guilt, one in which sins against chastity became the synonym for all sin. Moreover, from early childhood it was instilled into him that celibacy was the way of perfection as distinguished from marriage, the way of mediocrity. Naturally the challenge of "the greater" inspired him to join the seminary.

[10] *Chāndogya Upaniṣad*, II, 13, 1–2.
[11] *Bṛhad-āraṇyaka Upaniṣad*, VI, 4, 21.

But now in the maturer years of his life he realizes for the first time the positive value of sex as a mode of other-oriented self-transcendence and of interpersonal togetherness, which in no way hinders the quest after perfection. Such a reappraisal could not have taken place in the seminary, which he joined very young at the age of fourteen or fifteen, where he was taught to consider women as a potential danger to his vocation. With the new awakening, therefore, the psychological props to his original option for celibacy fall to the ground. In other words the person who has to practise celibacy today is almost qualitatively different from the one who opted for it, whether we consider his self-understanding or his understanding of the world. This is particularly true of India where one has to telescope, mentally if not materially, into a short span of, say, thirty years historical changes which in the West took centuries of gestation. As a result the priest has once again to find his moorings. Some do come out of this crisis strengthened in their original option. Others on the contrary come to the conclusion that they would only be respecting the historicity of God's call if they choose either to leave the priesthood or to marry and continue in their ministry. Of the persons we have interviewed almost all agree that if celibacy were made optional and if the authorities agreed to educate the faithful to welcome the change and give those concerned a family wage, a good many priests (the estimate varies from twenty-five to fifty per cent) of the middle and lower age groups would choose married priesthood.

3. An Ambivalent Witness

If obligatory celibacy as a witness to the kingdom of God was at no time unambiguous, today it is increasingly becoming the object of cynicism. Even in traditional India one believed that holiness or self-realization is to be achieved in the context of marriage. The lawgiver Manu taught that "the highest state", spiritual perfection, is attainable only to those who have successively gone through the four stages of life, those of the student, the householder, the forest-dweller and the ascetic.[12] He considers married life "the most excellent" since it is the support of all the other stages.[13] Besides, many of the great seers and saints of the

---

[12] Manu Smṛti, VI, 88.   [13] Ibid., VI, 89.

past like Yajñavalkya, Vyāsa and Vasiṣṭha, were married men. Neither was priesthood tied up with celibacy. For every householder was a priest in his own right.[14] The tradition of "brahmacarya" may not be adduced as a counter argument. For originally, and primarily, it meant chastity, i.e., conduct according to "brahman", which meant right knowledge.[15] Elsewhere the term is used to mean the stage of "studentship" preparatory to marriage. It is true that the term is also employed to signify the renunciation of marriage, which, however, formed only a marginal trend in Indian tradition, and was never considered the only or even the highest way of perfection.[16] Besides, as a rare and unique manifestation of the transcendence of the human spirit, celibacy included freedom of option as the mark of its authenticity. Hence the average Indian fails to appreciate a renunciation of marriage that is required by law. His initial reaction on seeing a Catholic priest is one of amused curiosity. Hence his usual question: "You are not allowed to marry, are you?" Seldom, if ever, does he ask: "Why did you give up marriage?" But today curiosity is giving place to disbelief and even cynicism among the more educated classes, especially in places where priestly celibacy has become a topic of discussion in the secular press. No less cynical is the attitude of certain sections of the faithful especially in south India. Here cynicism is further reinforced by the knowledge of the sexual deviations of priests. There is an enveloping climate of suspicion in which the younger clergy feel stifled and inhibited.

IV. Conclusion

Our analysis shows that the existing law, besides rendering doubtful the witness value of celibacy itself, is experienced by many priests in India as an obstacle in the way of their reorienting their lives in response to the call of God as revealed in the historically conditioned evolution of their self-understanding.

[14] *Yajñavalkya Smṛti*, I, 97–105; 115–16.
[15] *Praśna Upaniṣad*, I, 23.
[16] Hence nothing could be farther from the truth than the statement of Archbishop Padiyara in the synod: "It is difficult for the Hindu to think of some one as a man of God if he is not a celibate": cf. *Osservatore Romano*, No. 42 (186) (Oct. 1971), p. 5.

This aspect of the problem has been completely ignored by the Indian hierarchy. The latter has also failed to ascertain the real mind of the clergy. In our view the majority of the junior clergy favour optional celibacy.[17] All this shows that the present crisis is likely to persist, if not become aggravated in future. An adequate solution will be in sight only when all sections of the faithful hearken to God who in and through history speaks the truth that sets man free.

[17] I have intentionally not considered the question of the ordination of married men, since the only objection raised against it is that it would eventually lead to the abolition of celibacy. See the intervention of Archbishop Arulappa in the synod, *Osservatore Romano*, 45 (189), p. 6.

Adrian Hastings

Celibacy in Africa

"THE problem of the law of celibacy is one of the many problems which the young African churches are called to submit to a fresh examination." Such is the view of the clergy of Zaïre, as manifested in a report of 1970 produced by the episcopal subcommission for the clergy meeting with provincial delegates of the clergy.

The question of celibacy today is central to the whole future development of the institutional Church in Africa; indeed it is probable that without drastic changes here the Roman Catholic Church will not be able to avoid a major breakdown within a very few years.

As elsewhere, the question has been developing for a good many years though it is only very recently that it has really come to the fore; for a long time a policy of official repression has inhibited public discussion. Right back in the nineteenth century, Cardinal Lavigerie, writing towards the close of his life to Pope Leo XIII in a letter dated 1 July 1890, had proposed to Rome that there should be freedom for all African priests to marry. This suggestion was rejected by the Holy Office. The Western Church as a consequence imposed its own discipline of celibacy without any mitigation upon the African Church, and without any consideration as to whether the discipline of the Eastern Church might not, in view of the socio-cultural tradition of Africa, be more fitting. In African society there was traditionally next to no place for the unmarried person. As the tying of the priesthood to compulsory celibacy is essentially a relative matter, not a point of doctrine, it should on sound missionary principles

have been open to the possibility of adaptation, as Cardinal Lavigerie, the greatest Catholic missionary thinker of the nineteenth
century, clearly saw. In practice, however, neither on this nor
on many other points, were sound missionary principles much
considered. The decisive consideration was instead that of conformity with current Western discipline.

There was, then, no discussion of the matter until a few years
ago, when two things were starting to become ever more obvious:
one was that in most countries very few African priests were
being ordained in proportion to the number of Christians, in
spite of the very considerable efforts spent upon minor and major
seminaries; the other was that the whole shape of the ordained
ministry, as at present envisaged, with its celibacy, long years
of segregated academic education and subsequent pattern of segregated clerical life, was in serious ways unsuitable for rural Africa
—and by far the greater part of African society remains completely rural.[1] Whereas the need for some very fully educated
priests was not disputed, what appeared to be an equally great
need was for many other priests, less academically formed but
more integrated into village society, and undoubtedly in most
cases married. In fact, all over Africa many thousands of such
church ministers already exist: the catechists. They have, in truth,
to fill the sort of position that a village priest has occupied in
Europe for many hundreds of years, but present Western canon
law prevents any of them from being ordained.[2] By the time of
the Second Vatican Council it was therefore being suggested that,
in face of the extreme pastoral need, a start should be made with
the ordination to the priesthood of a selection of married catechists or other respected community leaders,[3] that the African
Church should in fact model its ministry in part upon that of the
Eastern Churches. This inevitably produced a strong reaction
in some quarters, but the hierarchy of Zambia (where there is a
particularly severe shortage of African priests) voted in 1968 to

[1] For the development of the priesthood in Africa see, in particular,
A. Hastings, *Church and Mission in Modern Africa*, chapter 6 (London,
1967); *id., Mission and Ministry*, chapter 9 (London, 1971).
[2] For the position of catechists in Africa, see A. Shorter and E. Kataza,
Missionaries to Yourselves: African Catechists Today (London, 1972).
[3] See A. Hastings, *AFER (African Ecclesiastical Review)*, October 1964;
T. Slaats, *AFER*, October 1965.

request Rome for permission to ordain married men. In reply they were told not to discuss the matter further.

In 1969, the Catholic Church in Tanzania undertook a whole year of study (The Seminar Study Year: SSY) upon its pastoral and missionary needs, culminating in a major meeting at Dar es Salaam in December. A number of the papers prepared for consideration proposed the ordination of married men to meet the ever more acute shortage of priests in rural areas. One of these papers was written by Fr Stephen Mbunga, rector of Peramiho major seminary and one of the most distinguished Tanzanian priests; he made his proposal within the context of the whole development of "Ujamaa" society in Tanzania: the formation of socialistically grounded village communities. In July 1970, however, the bishops of Tanzania rejected proposals for a married clergy of any kind, adding "Let it be clearly understood that we are unwilling to allow Tanzania to be made an experimental station for these ideas."[4]

In the same year 1970, on the other side of the continent, the hierarchies of five countries (Gabon, Chad, the Central African Republic, Congo-Brazzaville and the Cameroons) voted in favour of a request to Rome for permission to ordain married men as the only possible way "to answer the most elementary pastoral needs".

When the synod met in Rome in September 1971 to discuss this precise question, the position was as follows: a minority of African bishops was firmly in favour of the ordination of married men and clearly said so. These included Cardinal Malula of Kinshasa, Bishop Dayen of Chad and Bishop Sarpong of Kumasi, Ghana. Another minority was firmly against, following the lead of Cardinal Zoungrana. In between was (and is) the majority; those who are on the one hand afraid of ordaining men after a less lengthy training than that of the traditional seminary and of the possible financial consequences of having married priests when the Church is already very short of money, but who are on the other hand more and more conscious of the steadily deteriorating pastoral situation in most dioceses. It must be added, however, that in most countries no serious consultation was car-

4 See *AFER*, 1970, 4, p. 364.

ried out with priests and people before the synod. Indeed President Nyerere of Tanzania has been heard to remark that as a lay Catholic he might have been consulted, but was not, and furthermore that the celibacy of the clergy is, in his view, a chief reason why they do not really support his *ujamaa* policy. Again, in most places little attempt has been made by hierarchies to assess the coming ministerial needs of the Church in face of the population explosion and the decline of overseas missionaries, or to propose viable alternative policies to the ordination of married men.

In the last two years, however, the debate in Africa has become a very much wider one. It is now no longer concerned only with the ordination of married men, but with compulsory celibacy for any secular priest. Before the first meeting of the archbishops of all Africa, at Kampala in 1969, Cardinal Zoungrana declared that the celibacy issue was an example of an "imported question", introduced by foreigners; it was not a problem for Africans. In 1972 it would be quite impossible to repeat this with any degree of plausibility. It is today abundantly clear that it is an African problem, for at least two reasons: firstly, because Africans have already voted by simply not coming forward within the Catholic Church in any sufficient number to accept a celibate priesthood, so that the vast majority of Catholic Africans are being deprived of any sort of regular Eucharist as a result. Secondly, the law of celibacy is being increasingly and openly challenged by African priests and seminarists in many parts of the continent. It would be impossible at present to provide an adequate documentation for this movement, but the following examples are particularly significant.

In July 1971, a questionnaire was sent to the priests of Kampala archdiocese in Uganda, the diocese with probably the largest number of priests in Africa (about two hundred), and there were ninety-seven replies (forty-eight Ugandans, forty-nine expatriates). To the question "Should married laymen be ordained priests?" sixty-three replied in the affirmative, thirty-one in the negative. To the question "Should ordained priests be allowed to marry?" thirty-four replied affirmatively, sixty negatively. It was clear that among men over forty-five years of age a large majority replied negatively, while among those under forty-five the majority was in favour. This was true for both Ugandans and expatriates. The Ugandan Priests Association (a voluntary body, whose African-only membership may be towards a hundred) presented a memorandum to the episcopal conference in September 1971 strongly recommending that celibacy should become purely optional and that priests already ordained be allowed to marry and remain in the ministry. It declared that "free and open discussion of celibacy in Africa has been thwarted" and based its recommendations on many grounds, among them "a worsening shortage of priests", the necessity of freedom for the exercise of a true charism, the claim that "the most important reason why the majority of young men leave seminaries is mandatory celibacy", and the assertion that the present law is already "largely not observed" and has become a "scandal in the Church".

Perhaps it is only in Zaïre (until recently Congo-Kinshasa), the country with the largest number of priests and of dioceses in Africa, that the whole question has been openly discussed at a national level. In the consultation of the Congolese clergy over seventy-six per cent voted in favour of dissociating obligatory celibacy from the priesthood. The commission mentioned at the beginning of this article, which met in June 1970, produced an extensive report upon the whole subject of the priesthood in the Congo today. While fully respecting the vocation of celibacy, the large majority came to the following conclusions, in which it surely also speaks for many other priests throughout the continent: "We propose that the integral or total tradition of the Universal Church be accepted and not just partial traditions. For, the Latin tradition on the subject of celibacy not being the tradition of the Universal Church, the Fathers of the African Church of the Congo cannot bind this Church and future generations to a partial tradition of the Catholic Church. . . .

"Marriage for the Congolese priest will not be a devaluation of the priesthood, but a fulfilment of the ancestral priesthood within the Christian priesthood. In fact, according to African tradition, it is the father of the family who presides over the liturgy and is the intermediary, not only between living and dead, but also between men and God. We hope that research will continue in the young church of the Congo to discover its own physiognomy and personality, and that the distinction between the two vocations, to the priesthood on the one hand, and to celibacy on the other, be recognized as a fact.

"In other words, let it be left to each one, as he is moved by the Holy Spirit and the desire to serve Christ, and in accordance with his own possibilities, to have liberty of choice between the priest-hood with celibacy and the priesthood with marriage."

This does not signify that almost all African priests today desire a change in the law of celibacy; in fact, many remain strongly opposed to change. What it does signify is that there are at least two views and it would be quite deceptive to describe just one as "the African point of view": the whole issue has now been forcefully raised and the pastoral state of affairs is such that it can certainly no longer be brushed aside.